"What a pleasure and inspiration it is to read these pages... You and Mary Lee are two such very special and heartwarming women and this lovely memoir conveys that in full measure... Best of luck to you with this marvelous (and inspiring) endeavor!"
—Katherine V. Forrest, highly published and acclaimed author

"This is such a lovely memoir and tribute to Mary Lee. I am so pleased to see the progress you're making and to watch this beautiful work developing... I encourage you to keep writing and complete this inspiring manuscript... many blessings to you on this exciting journey!"
—Laurie Gray, award-winning author

"I know you're anxious to tell this beautiful story and share it with the world... Beautiful story—beautiful women."
—Connie Gorrell, creator of "Celebrating the Spirit of Women" Conferences

Pat,
Congratulations on such a wonderful accomplishment! You should be very proud of yourself for the energy, tenacity, creativity, and vulnerability you have shown in sharing such a powerful and personal story. Congratulations and well done!
—Teresa Bucher, Unity of Fort Wayne Spiritual Center

We Came Alive in '75!

The Pat and Mary Lee Story

Inspired by **Dr. Mary Lee Richeson**

Written by **Pat Deihl**

Rogue Books

Bedazzled Ink Publishing Company * Fairfield, California

978-1-939562-50-0 paperback
978-1-939562-51-7 ebook

Cover Design
by

TreeHouseStudio

Cover photo
David Kirk
Kirk Photography, Fort Wayne, Indiana

Rogue Books
a division of
Bedazzled Ink Publishing Company
Fairfield, California
http://www.bedazzledink.com

Dear Glenda and Jane,
May you have courage to love deeply,
wisdom to keep learning your life
lessons, and the joy of a transformed life!
Love, Pat Deike

For my dear Mary Lee,
whose sweet and unconditional love continues to transform me,
even after 40 years together and her physical death.

You're beginning to get to know me; I like
Mary Lee so much, I'd like you to get to
know her, too. I hope this book will help
you to do that.

Acknowledgments

I have many, many people to thank for planting seeds in my life which eventually would result in the creation of this book:

My mother, Lois Waterman Deihl, was a highly intelligent woman who would have thrived as a college student, but since she grew up during the worst of the depression years, it would have been financially impossible for her. Also, growing up as a young woman in the early 1900's made it socially unacceptable for her. We didn't know it at the time, but she did become a very effective teacher—to her five children. Every time we said something that was grammatically incorrect (or inappropriate,) she would correct us, and then wait for us to repeat it back to her correctly. This was how all of us learned to speak in an educated and intelligent manner, from the time we were very young. I've recently realized what a head start she gave us all in our schooling, and in life. I have sometimes been told that I have a certain gift for writing, and that has made my endeavor to author this book easier than it might have been. Thanks, Mom!

Gert Martin, who, many years ago was one of my first spiritual teachers, taught me a life-changing lesson when I shared with her that my love for Mary Lee was so strong, that if she died first, I planned to commit suicide to be with her. (" . . . I'd rather live in her world, than be without her in mine . . .") Gert gently but firmly informed me that if I cut my life short before it was my time, that I would just have to return in another lifetime, to begin again with all the problems and lessons I still needed to learn in this lifetime. I would gain nothing and would certainly find no relief by cutting my life short. In an instant, my suicide pact with myself suddenly disappeared from my mind and heart forever.

Gert also taught me that upon the death of a dearly loved one, I could choose to live out the rest of my life bitterly grieving my loss, or blame God, or be angry at the one who left me—or I could use that loss as a strong stimulus to experience phenomenal spiritual growth. That's the path I had already chosen, years before Mary Lee died.

After a horrendous car accident and Mary Lee's death, I'm grateful that two very good friends of ours, Beth Lauer and Nancy Kilduski, strongly advised me that as soon as I was physically recovered enough, I needed to get my choirs started again . . . "because they're your life." I did, and they were right.

The early morning of her death, I came home and sent an e-mail to both of our families, our friends, and our church, telling of my releasing her spirit to continue her journey. The first and most touching response I received came from Teresa Bucher, Unity's administrative assistant, who is also a minister. Her gentle but powerful words of support for the great gift I had just given to Mary Lee, which she said many people wouldn't have been able to give, brought me to tears but also comforted my heart.

Since that day, I have often had conversations with Teresa, learning many spiritual truths that I hadn't known before. She encouraged me, telling me that my spiritual growth, my new peace, was obvious to her and also to others in the church. She was my first grief counselor, my early comforter. Thank you, Teresa, for your sweet spirit.

I thank the members of both of my choirs, the Celebration Singers and the Festival Choir, for their love and support and for the music they made in my heart during that most difficult time; and today, their music still makes my spirit soar.

I thank members of both my family and also of Mary Lee's family, for their expressions of love, appreciation, and support of both Mary Lee and me during her life and also after her death. I'm especially grateful to my younger sister, Jan Blain, for travelling to be with me soon after the memorial service was over, because she knew I would greatly feel the lonely loss then; also, for sharing with me the unusual happenings shortly after that service; for being open to the veracity of what was occurring and especially for experiencing her own spiritual growth during this time.

I thank all of our dear friends at our church, now known as Unity of Fort Wayne Spiritual Center, who, on the very Sunday morning of her death, began the healing of my battered soul with gentle loving hugs, concern, and prayers for me. And now I am also blessed by our shared spiritual transformation, which has been guided by our transitional minister, our dear Rev. Barry Vennard.

I am in awe of the fans and also many of the stars at the Xena, Warrior Princess Conventions who identified with us, admired our fun and loving long-term relationship. Some even looked on us as role models to emulate, and often treated us like a very special couple, with love and respect. Many of them hugged me and cried when they heard that Mary Lee had died, and when I read a statement to the whole convention about her extremely alive and healthy soul's presence and her numerous interactions with me on a regular basis, they not only applauded, but also gave us a standing ovation! Several couples told me that what I had said had given them hope, learning that they didn't have to be separated by physical death.

I am grateful for the tiny seed planted by book publisher Claudia Wilde at the 2012 Xena Convention when she said to me, "You need to tell your story; you need to write a book about you and Mary Lee." When I demurred, she said I should write down my memories, and that they would help me—and they have. She and Casey have been so encouraging, informative, and gently helpful, that I feel like I now have two new, good friends at Bedazzled Ink.

I am profusely thankful to Laurie Gray, the award-winning author of three young adult novels: Summer Sanctuary, Maybe I Will, and Just Myrto, for the patient and incredibly generous advice and encouragement she gives me, and for sharing information about how to write a book even if you're not a professional writer. I feel highly privileged to have her as a friend, and also to have her write the foreword for this book.

I am grateful for the great gifts of Tina Zion, a fourth generation psychic who has helped me to be able to finally have conversations with Mary Lee and to interact with her. She has also helped me to move on with my grieving. Her gentle, caring attention and absolute faithfulness in repeating the exact words she hears from Mary Lee with their meaning, inflection, and even in describing Mary Lee's postures, hand gestures, and facial expressions, all of which have helped me to know that my Mary Lee is really there. Tina is a very gifted woman who freely shares her knowledge of the spirit world. She is enthusiastic and full of life, laughter, empathy, and comfort, and she has been teaching me to pay attention to subtle things that I never used to notice. She teaches all of us to learn to develop our own intuition and inner wisdom, to practice Living Aware, two words printed on her business cards and newsletters.

I thank Katherine V. Forrest, a prolific and highly gifted author/editor, and a wonderfully generous and loving friend to both Mary Lee and me for many years. We met her at a National Women's Music Festival in 1986, where we became new friends, and we have exchanged many letters and cards over the years. Katherine has consistently and eloquently spoken in such loving terms of us and of our relationship that we even kept a file labelled "Katherine V. Forrest," so that we could read and re-read the uplifting words she wrote to us.

I know that this section of a book is normally written to express thanks to people. But this morning I awoke, remembering that although I'd never meant to, I know that before I met Mary Lee, there were people in my life that I deeply hurt and possibly scarred. For that, I humbly ask your forgiveness.

I also know that Mary Lee fervently loved her daughter Jan and her son Joe, and in many conversations with me, she had shared her fear and regret for some things she had done in her past that had caused them both pain and anxiety, even anger. I believe that's why I woke up today thinking about the unwise things we each had done in our past, and of our hope for forgiveness.

My profound gratitude goes to my dearest Mary Lee, for as the words to a song from the musical *Wicked* declare, "Because I knew you, I have been changed for good." My sweet woman, even after your physical death, you continue to be my greatest teacher, helping me to find a new way of living, a new joy, and a confidence that I can indeed live a blessed and purposeful life even without having your physical presence by my side.

I'm also grateful for your habit of "whispering in my ear" as you stand behind my chair with your hands resting on my shoulders as I type this on the computer, and for being indeed, my very own . . . real, live ghost writer!

Every January, our church would sing "Happy Anniversary" to us. Sometimes, a couple would later come up to us and quietly say, "You are such an inspiration to us."

Foreword
by Laurie Gray

On Friday, November 14, 2008, Pat Deihl and Mary Lee Richeson welcomed me into their home in New Haven, Indiana. I was there to interview Mary Lee and write an article for our Unity newsletter. Having sung alto along with Mary Lee in Pat's Unity Christmas Choir the year before, I had spent some time with both of them and sensed that the love they shared was as deep as it was unpretentious. Seeing them together in their home, hearing them tell their stories, and feeling free to ask all of the questions I wanted under the guise of the interview, I received a rare glimpse into the private lives of Pat and Mary Lee.

The article, a mere 840 words, ran with the title "Dr. Mary Lee Richeson: Life Rocks!" in the January-February 2009 issue of the newsletter along with a picture of Mary Lee in her lapidary workshop. Mary Lee showed me a collection of rather dull, unimpressive rocks. Then she showed me how she would slab them into thin sections, grind, sand, and polish them, and transform them into precious stones.

"Each rock is a mystery," she told me. "You never know what's inside until you cut it open."

Mary Lee literally put the "jewel" in jewelry. She also loved to paint with oils and acrylics. For years Pat and Mary Lee's Christmas cards always included one of Mary Lee's creations. Her vibrant paintings of flowers and butterflies decorated the walls of their house. In a home filled with art and music, one painting was especially dear to Mary Lee. Using an old Brownie snapshot, Mary Lee painted her childhood home in Henryetta, Oklahoma.

Named after her mother (Mary Grace) and her father (Leroy), Mary Lee grew up on a dairy farm in Oklahoma during the Great Depression. "Those were hard times," she told me. She delivered milk with her older brother and two cousins, collecting the empty bottles, sterilizing them, and refilling them with raw milk. Mary Lee was the first in her family to graduate from high school, and she went on, earning her bachelor's degree from San Jose State and her master's degree in biology from Stanford.

In the seventies, while Mary Lee was teaching science labs at Indiana-Purdue University in Fort Wayne (IPFW), she began reading feminist literature. When her daughter Jan left for college and her son Joe was in high school, Mary Lee decided it was time to earn her doctorate so that she could become a full-time professor.

Mary Lee began anew in a small trailer in Muncie, teaching biology classes and science labs, doing research and completing her doctoral degree at Ball State. To help make ends meet, Mary Lee rented a room to a music teacher from New Haven who was studying at Ball State for the summer. Mary Lee found more than a renter; she found a whole new life with Pat Deihl. Their relationship grew from roommates to best friends and confidantes to soul mates. I'll always remember the gleam in Mary Lee's eyes and the smile on her face when she told me, "We fell in love."

Soon I was standing in their family room, amidst a vast array of *Xena Warrior Princess* memorabilia, each keepsake inspiring a new tale or anecdote from the many Xena Conventions they shared together over the years, their epic love mixing with the legend and lore that is Xena. Needless to say, I gained a whole new appreciation for the Mary Lee and Pat I'd met at Unity!

In July of 2010, I was stunned to learn of their automobile accident, and deeply saddened by the physical and legal barriers Pat faced as she tried to heal from her own serious injuries and struggled to spend every possible moment with Mary Lee, who was hospitalized with traumatic brain injuries. Through the rest of the summer, Pat and Mary Lee were limited to short visits and phone conversations. I was very blessed to visit with them both during that time and to witness firsthand how their love endured through sickness as it had in health.

Mary Lee suffered a massive stroke and her heart stopped beating on September 5, 2010. But that is not the end of this love story. Their hearts remain as one, and Mary Lee has been Pat's inspiration, muse, and "ghost writer" as Pat has worked diligently to create this book, inviting the world to share their spiritual, physical, and emotional journey together.

Pat Deihl and Mary Lee Richeson were together for thirty-six years on this earth, but their love is universal and eternal. *We Came Alive in '75* stands as a tribute to their transforming kind of love. Like Mary Lee's common-looking stones, this memoir is a mystery. The only way to discover the beauty inside is to crack it open and see for yourself.

Laurie Gray is the founder of Socratic Parenting LLC and the award-winning author of four books, including the gender-bending, young adult novel Maybe I Will.

Contents

Prologue (Before Our Lives Intersected) ❧ 15

Chapter 1
Three Kisses ❧ 23

Chapter 2
How We Began; Then, How We REALLY Began ❧ 27

Chapter 3
Letters, Letters, Cards, and Letters . . . and "Dings" ❧ 31

Chapter 4
Our First Decade: Good, Bad, and Ugly—and Better ❧ 47

Chapter 5
Second Decade: New Traditions Are Begun ❧ 62

Chapter 6
Third Decade: Party, Wedding, and Xena ❧ 73

Chapter 7
Fourth Decade: Party, Rainbow Room, Horror, Devotion ❧ 89

Chapter 8
A New Beginning: Butterflies, Birds, and Bunnies ❧ 115

Chapter 9
Shocking and Amazing Information (Read If You Dare!) ❧ 127

Chapter 10
Our Life Together Progresses . . . and Continues On ❧ 134

Epilogue
What's in Our Future? ❧ 146

About Pat Deihl ❧ 153

Songs My Mary Lee Has Sent to Me ❧ 155

Suggested Readings ❧ 162

Pat and her sister, Jan Blain, liked to wear one of their "sister shirts" when they visited each other.

Prologue

Our lives before we knew each other existed

Five generations of Radebaughs;
Mary Lee is born.

Mary Lee as a young woman.

With younger sister Eula Mae (Tudee),
and older brother Theon. (Youngest brother,
Tommy was deceased)

Her childhood was filled with poverty and a broken family early on.
She was the salutatorian of her high school graduating class—
She should have been the valedictorian, since she had the top grades.
However, a board member played politics and declared that
his daughter had that top honor, instead.

Grew up in the Nazarene Church—*very* strict, ultra-conservative religion.
She always dreamed of becoming a medical doctor, but had no financial
mentors to be able to enter medical school.

Twenty-nine years of being a traditional wife and mother, always striving
to be the very best at whatever she did.

Even years later, she feared dying alone, an impoverished old woman.

Oct.29, 1939—Patricia Jean Deihl is born in Indianapolis, Indiana

Moved to Fort Wayne, Indiana in 1940

Pat's Mom and siblings
Bob, Pat, Mom holding Margie, Bud, Jan in
front

Her childhood was filled with emotional detachment,
and stuffing down her feelings with food.

As a child she feared spankings
As an adult she feared being alone all her life.

She was also the salutatorian of her high school graduating class.
The teachers felt Pat should have been the valedictorian instead.
A glitch in the X,Y,Z lanes of classes.

Grew up in the American Baptist church—the most liberal
of all the types of Baptist denominations.

Thirty-five years of being self-hating, moody, feeling unlovable,
and unworthy of a happy life.

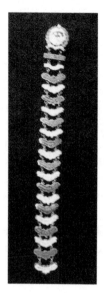

Pat's 22 year perfect attendance pin, given from 1943-65, when she last lived in Fort Wayne, moved to New Haven, and began attending another church.

1953 newspaper photo of us with our minister,wearing our "perfect attendance pins."
Pat, Margie, Dr. Lansing, Bob, Jan, Bud
[Photo courtesy of the *News Sentinal*, Fort Wayne, IN]

Pat's siblings, taken in 1997.
Bob Deihl, Jan Blain, Pat Deihl, Bud Deihl, Margaret Waite

THEN, in 1973

September

- Mary Lee and I met in a support group which had grown from six people to twenty!
- I was not happy—it was too big for everyone to report in.
- Mary Lee joined the group when it was quite large.
- We noticed each other in a non-personal way.
- Mary Lee said later that she was intrigued by me and looked forward to seeing her come in—usually late and taking a seat on the floor.
- I was depressed and afraid of the direction my life seemed to be headed.
- My weight was way up from lots of emotional eating, and I wore the same brown outfit every week, because it was the only thing large enough to fit me at that time.

November

- Mary Lee was leaving the group, and after her last session, as we stood in the parking lot by our cars, she handed me a small slip of paper on which she had written her full name and phone number.
- She was very aware of putting her hand on the shoulder of my black winter coat. I was oblivious to it.
- I sent Mary Lee a Christmas card, so that now she also had my full name, address and phone number.

December

- We met at Azar's Restaurant and talked for over an hour.
- Mary Lee was convinced that I wanted to meet and marry a man.
- I was convinced I would never find anyone who would love me. I wanted to be normal and be loved, but didn't see that in my future.
- Neither communicated her thoughts to the other at that time.

1974

December

- Mary Lee sent me a Christmas card, inviting me to meet at Azar's again.

Recently, I found Mary Lee's partial autobiography, which she had typed onto our ancient Apple IIe computer (we had purchased it around 1985.) I saw that she had written it in 1995, shortly after her retirement from IPFW, when she finally had time to compose it from her memories of her young life. She had intended to write more, also listing "Learning, Marriage, Motherhood, Reinventing Life, and Making It." She never got around to those.

I was not aware that she had written this until I had discovered it after her death.

I'm copying most of the words she wrote about her early years. It shows me why, even as an adult, she still feared ending up old, alone, and in poverty once again.

MY BIOGRAPHY—EARLY YEARS
Mary Lee Richeson

I don't remember being born, as some have claimed, but I can recall being two when I got a red rocking chair from Santa. We lived out on the Old Farm then, but I was born in a house at the east foot of "Bald Knob" hill, on January 15, 1925. The family moved to the dairy farm out south of Henryetta sometime before I was two or three. The farmhouse was simple in construction without closets, we had large draperies over the corner of the bedrooms to stand behind to put on clothes. I used to hide from Mama in there when she called. My dad got up early and milked cows and delivered milk in an old Dodge truck to people somewhere. My brother Theon had his tonsils out when I was three (he was four, eleven months difference in age) and that is the first time I remember getting part of a Hershey chocolate bar, a wonderful memory!

Mama cooked a lot and entertained preachers on Sundays. It was at one of these Sunday dinners, when I, sitting politely and sweetly at my place made a "famous" embarrassing remark when my innards made audible and rumbling sounds in response to my hunger. I spoke up and said something to the effect, "Excuse me, my bowels just moved." Mama told that story on me many times later, with great laughter.

We had an Essex, a great car, and on the way back from the hospital with Theon after his tonsillectomy, we had to cross a dangerous railroad crossing; the trains ran so fast and from around a curve and a hill. We stopped and listened but could not hear, but Theon did because of some acuteness in his ears and so we waited, and sure enough, that fast train would have surely hit us and my brother got credit for saving the whole family.

I had a pair of red boots and often waded in the muck of the dairy. Once, I fell down with them on and jabbed a place on my cheek. The scar looked like the dimple I never had but wanted because of Shirley Temple. I was not wearing them, but was barefoot (most of the time) the summer I saw a hen lay an egg. I was actually in the hen house (forbidden to bother the layers) and scared one off her nest and she proceeded to stop and grunt one out. I squatted down and observed the whole process, an amazing revelation which whetted my interest in biological events and influenced my entire life.

When I was about four or five we pretty much had the run of the farm, climbing fences and playing in the hay barn which was in sight of the house. I had male cousins, but no female ones, so I was very much a tomboy and held my own readily.

When I became five, Theon six, we had to move

to town so we could be put in school. By then, the Radebaugh Dairy which my dad ran with Uncles Guy and Ed, had broken up (or gone broke because the depression had started.) Times became difficult. The land on north 16th Street was deeded to my dad by my grandfather. There were about 120 acres at first, of good land that was suitable for cattle and a place for a pond to be constructed. A house was moved overland from Kusa. It cost $120 and was put in place where "the old home place" stands today. There were no porches, and of course, no bathroom. I had not lived in a house with a bathroom, so it seemed a really great thing to have, a house with four rooms and gas lights.

We moved there in about 1930 and Daddy had twelve cows and started to build a milk route. They build a milk house for bottling milk, and there was a barn down on the other side of the pond. It was a great place for kids; we had Tudee by then, about one or two years old.

I started school when I was six (no kindergarten then) at Irving Elementary and we had to walk. My teacher was Miss Davidson and I got stars reading The Gingerbread Man and Little Black Sambo. The principal was Miss Embree and she looked very stern. Sometimes we had to go to the principal's office and get down on our knees and put our head in her lap while she searched our hair for head lice nits, a practice bound to spread them, I would think. I never had them, but I lived in fear and was warned about using other kids' combs.

I was never the most popular kid, but I was always the best scholastically, a pattern that I had most of my school life. When I was in elementary school every girl wanted to look like Shirley Temple, but my hair was black and very straight—so much for that. By the time I was in 3rd grade, President Roosevelt had been elected and the depression was intense. My dad could not make a go of the dairy; it must have been bad. To make it, my father decided to sell out and to move

to north of town with us, leasing out our home place for a year. Daddy ran a dairy for Dr. McKinney, and I went to Webster School. We lived a mile north of the top of 5th Street hill and I had to walk to school, and walk home. We were living there when I was ten years old; I remember because that is when my mother told me about menstruation. It was scary. She said I should be on the lookout for bleeding and not take any cold baths because that could cause serious consequences.

As things went from bad to worse in our financial situation, we moved from the house at Dr. McKinney's farm to a place in Gillam Addition. I remember having to help deliver milk from a horse and buggy. Things had gone backward, no more car or truck— back to horses. We lost a lot, like most people did in the 30's. For a while Daddy worked for the WPA and Mama worked in a sewing room. It was at this time that Mama took a beauty course and learned to give perms and facials. She opened a beauty shop in Henryetta, but it must have failed.

Our family was coming apart and both parents drank and went to parties. We did not go to church anymore. I remember vividly the big fight one night, when my father raged at my mother with a huge butcher knife. I surmised she had told him she was pregnant and that the father of the child was another man. They must have made their bargain with that, because Mama had my brother, Tommy Radebaugh; my mother did not forgive herself, and my father never forgave her and did not forget it. My younger brother suffered his entire life as a result of the differential treatment from my parents.

My sequencing is off. I choose not to remember some of it; we moved a lot and then I remember my father decided to go to the CCC camp somewhere in Colorado. There were four of us; brother Tommy was sickly and we all had poor nutrition. We lived in a big two-story house, just south of the courthouse, and I was in the 6th grade. This was the winter that Flora Archer, my teacher, gave me a coat. I remember it was still hard to keep warm walking to school. Mama was drinking and her acquaintances were not the best quality. It was at this house that one day I drank a half glass of orange gin on a dare, not knowing what it was like. Nobody cared what I did. I learned lots about the seamy side of people, the ugliness of neglect and the worst poverty I have ever known.

We couldn't make do with the allotment check from the CCC camp ($22.50 per month for the five of us) and I prefer not to think about how we all survived. We were often sick, cold (in the winter), and hungry. When we were finally able to move back to our house on the hill, it was at least our own home, so when Mama's boyfriend stole chickens for us to eat, it seemed like a good idea.

In the summer of 1936 Mama took Tommy and me and took off with her boyfriend for California in an old Pontiac. We stole gas and tires and anything else and arrived in the LA area, much to the disgust of our relatives. Tommy and I were abandoned, turned over to juvenile authorities, and finally sent back to Oklahoma by the state, accompanied by my Grandmother Sanders. Mama landed in a Phoenix jail, turned state's evidence, and came back to Henryetta later that winter. All of us kids were in the custody of foster parents. It was a very low time.

Those years and the ones that followed were traumatic for me and for all the family. One never quite gets over it, and so one survives the best one can. The next year, Mama took all four of us kids and we went back to our house on the hill. We had no furniture, just one wooden chest. We had to pry the wooden barricades from the doors where my Dad had boarded up the house. He had sold every single possession at public auction. And so my Mother, with grit and sober determination, held on and we held together. I credit my Mother with our survival, both as a family, and as individuals. My Dad was "still away." He eluded his responsibility from the time I was about ten years old until I left home after high school.

This was a synopsis of my early years.

Chapter 1
Three Kisses

Kiss #1

". . . Oh, oh, she had kisses sweeter than wine"

Early in our relationship, Mary Lee asked me, "How many times do you think we've kissed?" Without a moment's hesitation, I responded, "Not enough!"

In January, 2010, at the conclusion of a choir rehearsal in our home, it was party time! Mary Lee sang alto in both of the choirs that I direct, and she just had her eighty-fifth birthday, so we were going to have a surprise celebration in her honor, complete with ice cream, a decorated cake with candles, singing, and lots of visiting and enjoying the company of one another—something this choir does, even when it's not someone's birthday.

But wait! Her eighty-fifth birthday was January 15, and on January 9 was also our thirty-fifth anniversary—so the cake reflected both dates, with one lit candle for each five years. Fifteen years before, when we actually had used seventy candles on one cake and twenty on the other, there were remarks of "Turn off the lights, we don't need them!" and "Hurry, the frosting's melting!" and "Where's the nearest fire marshal?"

We all sang to Mary Lee, then the choir sang "Happy Anniversary" to both of us, as we joined in and sang to each other, then kissed. We didn't know until later that Matt, one of our choir members, had taken both pictures. We used them on the cover of a CD that we made several months later.

Kiss #2

"Whither Thou Goest, I Will Go " (sung at our wedding by Jan Davis, Mary Lee's daughter)

On January 8, 2000—the day before our twenty-fifth anniversary—we had a formal Joining Ceremony—created by us—in the sanctuary of our own Unity Christ Church, with two ministers, members of both of our families, and two dear friends all taking part in the ceremony, with a professional photographer, and over a hundred loving friends and family members in attendance. Later, our Celebration Singers Choir kept insisting on referring to it as our wedding. We finally gave up and agreed on their terminology.

Both choirs have continued to love, respect, and honor us and our relationship. No big change in how they related to us, they just came to know us better from that event. They have continued to be relaxed and absolutely supportive of our loving relationship.

I didn't think that ceremony would change anything for us, since we'd already been together for twenty-five years. But I was wrong! Standing up in front of our friends and families as we declared our love for each other in public for the first time, kissing each other in front of a lot of people for the first time, and having them applaud and cheer us as they stood up in support of us . . . Everything was different from that point on!

Kiss #3

In February, 2009 we attended our tenth Xena, Warrior Princess national convention in California, along with more than a thousand other fans. We had been enjoying seeing old friends and taking part in many exciting activities over the four days, meeting people we didn't even know, who said things like,

"We're so relieved to see you both here this year; we were afraid you might not be back, since last year you both were using canes."

And . . .

"I took this picture of you dancing together last year and hoped I would have a chance to give you this copy if I saw you."

And . . .

"You make these conventions so much fun for us!"

And from a book publisher . . .

"I so enjoyed talking to you at last year's Xena Con."

And from Gary, one of the three organizers of the conventions . . .

"You guys are a large part of the fond memories I hold of the Xena Conventions."

And . . .

"You are such a role model for other couples . . . how long you've been together, and still you so obviously love doing things together, and you still have such fun together!"

We've been treated like adored mini-celebrities there, even by some of the stars and celebrities from the show. Traveling was becoming more difficult for us, and we'd even wondered if maybe we should not try to attend anymore. We finally determined that it was one of the highlights of our year, the best, most affirming, uplifting, fun thing we did each year, and that we'd keep coming just as long as we were able to.

There was a panel on the stage discussing a movie they'd made recently, called Bitch Slap (don't even ask!) and one of the main stars of the Xena TV show—Renée O'Connor, who had played Xena's sidekick, Gabrielle—made an unexpected entrance down the center aisle, wearing a nun's costume, from her role in the movie.

"I love how your eyes close whenever you kiss me . . ."

The panel answered questions from the audience, and the moderator eventually said, "We have time for just one more question. If someone can ask a really outrageous question, we'll give you this packet containing pictures of all the characters in the movie."

I got a mischievous idea and asked Mary Lee to stand up with me. We were seated in row four, center aisle. Mary Lee knew I was up to something, but she also knew that I would never humiliate her, so she complied.

I said to the panel, "We don't have an outrageous question, but we do have an outrageous act."

Then I whispered in Mary Lee's ear, "Trust me," as I slid my arm around her waist. She turned toward me as I embraced her and planted a long, long, long, passionate Hollywood-type kiss on her mouth, as she returned my embrace and enthusiastically entered into the kiss.

Even with our eyes closed, we were aware of many, many flashbulbs going off during our kiss, as the fans stood and cheered, laughed, and applauded, and took numerous pictures of us. Talk about bringing the crowd's energy level up with a bit of fun!

When things quieted down some, the moderator handed us the packet of photos and said, "For that, you deserve two packets of photos . . . and we'd like to interview you both later!"

Three kisses . . . We had no idea that 2010 would be our last Xena Convention together.

Chapter 2
How We Began . . .

"Just in Time, I found you just in time . . ."

But . . . what about our relationship? How and when did it begin and develop and ultimately transform us both?

Back in September, 1973, I was a member of a therapy group led by Dr. H a psychologist who was trying to heal some troubled people who had a wide variety of problems, some more devastating than others. He was so impressed with our encouraging support of one another that he kept adding more and more people to the group, hoping they could find help there.

How Pat looked when she first met Mary Lee

I was one of the original five or six; I was there because I wasn't happy with my life or with myself. I didn't like where I seemed to be heading. Now that the group had grown to almost twenty people, too large to even check in with each person, I was disgruntled, as he introduced yet one more new person to the group.

I remember as I watched her every week, she was thoughtful, intelligent, and soft spoken, a voice of reason. She was always dressed professionally, with a decorative pin covering the top button of her blouse, which was often covered by a long vest. She evidently had a husband who was quite troubled. She also eventually shared that she wanted to explore something she had been awakened to recently. She told me much later that she had always waited for me to come in and was intrigued by me.

How Mary Lee looked when she first met Pat

In November, she told the group that this was her last session, and that she wouldn't be attending anymore. The group told her that she was fine, that she didn't need the therapy, but her husband did. We felt he was the one needing treatment in that family.

When we went to our cars at the end of that session, she handed me a little slip of paper with her name and phone number on it, in case I wanted to call her. (I was so naïve!) She later sent me a Christmas card, I called her, and we decided to meet at a restaurant for coffee and talk.

We talked for over an hour, and she surmised that what I wanted in life wasn't what she wanted. We had no communication for a year, while she worked at a university in another city, in pursuit of her doctoral degree.

Then, in December of 1974, she sent another Christmas card to me, suggesting that we meet again and talk. I just recently was astonished to find the original handwritten note she had sent me, dated December 1, 1974.

After that meeting, as we returned to our cars, she referred to women like us. I looked sharply at her and said defensively, "What do you mean, women like us?" She backed off, and we said goodbye—again.

After I got home, the phone rang and she asked if I was okay and that she hoped she hadn't offended me. Her manner and words were disarming, and I felt more relaxed and comfortable, less pressured, and appreciative of her kind understanding.

Dear Pat,

  Have thought of you many times and wondered how you are.

  Do you still attend group?

  I am at Ball State working on my doctorate—am now in residency, but will be home for Christmas after Dec. 20th. Would you be game for a cup of coffee at Azars on the Highway (as before) say, about Dec. 23, at 1 pm? That's on Monday. If not—drop me a note at Muncie, Indiana.

  See you.

  Mary Lee Richeson

  P.S. Have had some interesting experiences.

A few days later, she phoned me, in great distress. I hesitated, and then invited her up to my apartment, because I understood the pain of her situation. Since I knew she couldn't confide in anyone else, we talked, and I comforted her. We didn't know it then, but through grieving, empathy, and compassion, our relationship-to-be was being born.

Soon, we were in separate cities, so we began exchanging phone calls and almost daily letters, and at one point she wrote "I think we should explore our senses of humor—I think we will laugh a lot." And we did continue to explore, enjoy, and bring joy and laughter to each other and those around us for the next thirty-six years.

In one phone call, I said to her, "I don't know why what you write or say matters so much to me, but it really does." In the first week of January, 1975, Mary Lee had said that she'd come to visit me the following weekend. I said "I'd like that." But inside, I was actually jumping up and down and ecstatic. A few days later, when she mentioned off-handedly that she wouldn't be coming, I was swept with sadness and greatly disappointed, nearly in tears. Why did it matter so much?

That's how we first met.

Now, when did we really begin our relationship?

And on what did we base the date of our anniversary for the rest of our many years together?"?

Then, how we *really* began.

How we REALLY Began . . .

> *"Something Tells Me I'm in for Something Good"*
> *"Oh, What a Night!"*
> *"You Made Me So Very Happy"*

On Thursday, January 9, 1975, I was taking a shower before going to bed, when my phone rang. No cell phones then, no cordless phones, no caller ID—So I got out of the shower with my completely soaped-up body, picked up the phone, and was amazed and delighted to hear her voice as I stood there dripping soap and water all over the floor. She asked if I would be interested in driving down to Muncie and spending the weekend with her, and if it might be possible for me to come this same evening.

I said, "Yes, as soon as I get rinsed and dried and pack a few things and arrange for a substitute for my Friday classes, (I called in sick before I left,) I'll be on my way." Talk about adrenaline! And moving fast! And tossing a few things into a small bag: toothbrush, toothpaste, change of clothes, pajamas, and giddily throwing it into my car, as I joyfully began my journey to her.

I was enjoying the cold evening, seeing patches of snow in the fields (the highway itself was clear all the way) as I drove toward the truck stop where we'd arranged for us to meet. I had an awareness that I was beginning to move toward a new adventure, not knowing what was going to happen. Still a bit naïve, huh? She led me to a Travel Lodge in the town, and when I unpacked my pajamas, she grinned and said, "I don't think you'll be needing those."

> *"It's Too Late to Turn Back Now . . .*
> *I believe, I believe, I believe I'm fallin' in love . . ."*

At one point, she asked if I was ever going to kiss her on her mouth. I hadn't felt ready, and she didn't push it. My reply was, "Soon, maybe soon. I don't know." Before very long, I kissed her on the lips . . . and then, again . . . and again . . . and . . .

Several hours later, she pleaded, "Honey, I have a lecture to give at the university at eight a.m. tomorrow morning, and I really need to get some sleep. Can you stop kissing me for a little while?"

I responded as I kissed her, "I couldn't kiss you on the mouth for a long time . . . and now that I've begun, I can't stop!"

She chuckled, and turned over, and I kissed her several more times on her shoulders, neck, and upper back, before I relented and we both finally got a little bit of joyful, exhausted, and peaceful sleep before morning.

This is the date that we observed as our anniversary, for it was the first of many, many times that one of us would drive miles and miles to be with the other, for the next three-and-a-half years. By the spring of 1978, I had purchased a home near the school where I taught, and she had completed her work at the university and was now Dr. Mary Lee Richeson! No more long drives or motels for us. We finally had our own home together.

Ironically, folded inside that original 1974 note, I found another note, dated Christmas, 1975 (sent December 21.) She would have written this one after we'd been together for a year; notice the different tenor of this note, compared to the earlier one, from the salutation to the sign-off:

Dear One,
I looked it up on my '74 calendar and it was on Dec. 23, 1974, and one o'clock at Azar's on the highway that we met and commenced this madness between us. I wanted to know for sure. It was on Monday.
This year Dec. 23 comes on Tuesday. Let's try to meet at one o'clock at Azars on the highway. I hope we can.
Our anniversary, sort of.
*   I hope to see you there.*
*   You are my heart, my hope.*
*   My love*

Chapter 3
Letters, Letters, Cards and Letters . . . and "Dings"

"I Just Called To Say . . . I Love You"

Since back in the 1970s, we had to pay for every long-distance phone call, we would often arrange to ding each other, usually sometime during the evening. One of us would hear the phone ring just once, and *not* pick up; then the other one would answer by doing the same thing back. It was our secret (and free) way of communicating each evening when we were in different cities—even in later years, we would do this when long-distance calls cost.

No cell phones or e-mail yet, either—the stone age of communication.

Um . . . Mary Lee has strongly suggested that I leave out the most personal/passionate parts of these letters, since they were never meant to be read by anyone else. So the lascivious parts have been heavily redacted, so that none of our family or friends—or even strangers—will be embarrassed or uncomfortable.

One day during the last week of December 1974, Mary Lee had called me in great distress, was hesitantly invited and came over to my apartment and was gently comforted. She had expressed great apprehension about a New Year's Eve party they would be hosting in their home, with the other person present.

I told her I would call her during the party, ask for her, and then say something really outrageous to her to shock her and make her laugh, so she could get through the evening, knowing that I was there for her. A few days later, she came to my place again and we realized that we were gradually becoming very important to one another.

We never waited to answer each other's letters. We simply wrote to each other virtually every day that we weren't in the same city. These are mostly excerpts of our first six months of correspondence in 1975, from January through early June, when we could finally be together in Muncie during the summer. Notice how quickly our formal salutations and sign-offs changed.

P—Sunday, January 5
[Written just after Mary Lee had driven back to Ball State University, in Muncie, Indiana.]

Hi!

Hope you had a good trip back; sorry I didn't get a chance to talk to you. I was in and out all day, trying to do 3 loads of laundry and running home in between, in case the phone might ring. (Did ya' get a chance to try to call?) . . .

Hey, how about if you check into what's going on there the weekend of Fri, the 17th? Maybe we can work out something for then. (Already doing lots of thinking about it.)

By the way, excuse my many incomplete sentences—I think you can still understand what I'm saying, and it takes up less room, right? Right!

I don't believe how soon I began writing my first letter to you—the very day you left! . . .

Don't feel like you have to answer this right away—if we start shooting letters back and forth so frequently, we'll never get anything else done! (grin) I don't practice what I advocate, do I? (smile)

Write you again later!

ML—Monday, January 6

Thanks for being around. Your understanding and sympathy meant, and still means, very much.

I tried to call you yesterday—several times—wanted badly to say goodbye and that I was thinking of you.

I wish we had had more time to talk, to get to know each other, to explore . . . I will contact you somehow . . . I want very much for us to get together for an hour or two.

    With sincere regards and interest always yours—

ML—Tuesday, 1/7
After a phone call

Dear,

Talking with you was great; I like the sound of your voice, for a number of reasons . . . Have been feeling really good about things. Hope you are OK, too.

    With love

ML—Wednesday, 1/8

Your letter both surprised and pleased. Don't think for a minute you are fooling anyone with your coy and inventive words! I know what you are talking about and I must say that I did not suspect that you are something of a tease. And a rather obvious one at that!

I hope you will not mind if I am a bit more subtle . . .

The following poem is by Brown . . .

My voice rings down through thousands of years
to coil around your body and give you strength,

You who have wept in direct sunlight,
Who have hungered in invisible chains,
Tremble to the cadence of my legacy:
An army of lovers shall not fail.

Read carefully, breathe deeply and take heart. "Neither be cynical about love; for in the face of all aridity and disenchantment it is perennial as the grass."
There is a caring that dispels disenchantment. But there is risk. We will be careful. I hope that the weeping in direct sunlight will give way to a secret and joyous expectancy.

    Yours

P—Wednesday, 1/8

Hi!

Such a surprise, to get a second letter already! Such a NICE surprise—especially when I saw how you began it and ended it . . . gave me a good feeling.

I've been thinking about the possibility of using a "personal leave day" to come down some weekday to see you; we might even have a couple of days and nights that way. We'll save that idea as a possibility to consider later—maybe in the spring? (We'll see)

Talk to you later, Dear.

> *"Can't Help Myself, I Fall in Love with You"*

On Saturday, Jan. 11, during a phone call, at one point, I hemmed and hawed around and finally hesitantly said, "Uh, I kinda think . . . I think I love you . . . I'm pretty sure that I love you." I was never very good at identifying my emotions, but I knew my feelings for Mary Lee were very strong, and very positive.

ML—Saturday, 1/11

You have my head spinning. What you said on the phone was more than I expected, but very wonderful to hear. Please do not feel that you must say anything. What we do is expression enough.

I am personally very insecure. We should go slow . . . I look upon our friendship as a fulfilling and exciting experience . . .

Your smile is beautiful and it makes me happy to see you so lively and mischievous. I think we should explore our senses of humor, I think we will laugh a lot. I am looking forward to seeing you.

Sincerely yours

P—Saturday, 1/11

When you lust after someone, would you say you're feeling "lusty"? Oh, well—

Lustingly yours—

P—Monday, 1/13

Hi, I betcha!   (How 'bout that for a salutation?)

What's the opposite of a heartache? That's what I've got. A happy heart? That sounds right. Hey, do me a favor, ok? Be patient with me when I get too ornery or too exhuberant, ok? (I'm not promising to stop, I just want you to be patient.)

By the way, just to set the record straight; what I said on the phone (just before we hung up last Saturday) was not because I felt I must—I said it 'cause I couldn't keep from saying it. (It would bother me though, if you felt obligated to respond.) I'm sorry for pushing; I don't mean to.

When I first started to get to know you a little bit (over a year ago,) I felt as if you were someone I'd like to know better, as if you could be kind of a special person to me. But I never guessed how it would—how it could be. Know what? You're really a neat person! I think I'll go to sleep with that thought in my mind. Time to call it a day. (a night?)

G'night.

ML—Monday, 1/13

Dear friend and co-luster,

Sensational! Got two letters today. I really enjoyed both of them, including your obvious tongue-in-cheek and successful attempt at cuteness. You are cute, you know. A little "strange" but nevertheless cute and clever.

I especially feel free when I am with you—thank you for your friendship. I hope it grows, and grows.

As you remember, it is quite a stretch and the road is narrow there, do be extra careful. You are important to me. Ok? . . . Wish you were here, or would call . . . I would tell you what is in my heart, if you were here. Please play it cool, dear one.

Yours

P—Tuesday, 1/14

Hi again, Dear One!

I'm always pleased when you call, but it was even more beautiful that you called me when you were feeling down. I hope I was able to help a little.

I miss you. Can't wait to get the next letter . . . to talk to you on the phone . . . to finally see you. Get bunches of work done today and tomorrow, so that the time passes faster, and so we can maybe have a more relaxed, leisure time together, ok?

Have a good day, Dear!
See you shortly.

[*January 15 is ML's birthday. On that day, Mary Lee sent me this poem:*]

> *Just to say that I am thinking of you*
> *In the most positive way.*
>
> *My joy and anticipation go beyond*
> *The usual reasons*
>
> *To get to know you better as a person*
> *To laugh and be happy, to share*
> *A common identity.*
>
> *No matter where we are going together*
> *Or for how long*
> *The time will seem too short.*

[*I sent Mary Lee a card:*]

For your BIRTHDAY: Your very own set of MATCHED LUGGAGE!!!!!
Inside—2 teeny-weeny 2-inch by 5½ inch paper bags, with "for toothbrush" written under one, and "for make-up" under the other.

Then, in one of the little sacks, I put a tiny folded note.

On the front I printed "Hi, Dear One!"
Inside, the left side read:

My Love, You asked me if I would be a stable part of your life—
well, here's part of my birthday gift for you—
You are already an irreplaceable part of my life,
and I expect you to be that for a long, long time.
To even contemplate being without you makes me sad.
To think of your nearness makes me very happy!

On the right side, I printed:

Here's my wish for your new year:
May it be a year full of many accomplishments from your hard work,
many joys from your friends,
much peace and serenity when it's most needed, and most of all
May you have, minute by minute, that serenity and security which come
from knowing that you are deeply and steadfastly loved.

ML—Monday, 1/20

Of course we have gone much farther (and faster) than I ever thought we would. The prospects are immensely interesting and filled with anticipation . . . Both of us seem to have flipped in a most wonderful way. Might it all be too good to be true?

It's also wonderful, fantastic, beautiful, warm, alive, exciting, and far-out. And good . . .

I can't imagine what will happen now. It's all so great I'm thinking it will all be downhill from here on.

Only . . .
I don't think so.

There obviously has been something like it before, somewhere, with some other people. But I have never heard of it.

Poets, I know, write lots about it. But they didn't know about us. Strange,

The complete joy with you is more than I had hoped for.

Please don't go away
(You're beautiful!)

ML—(same day—5 pm)

So cold and snowy here, but the sun is shining brightly—a dim imitation of my own secret inner glow!

Have set aside this time for writing to you. I feel you so close, yet, often I realize I don't really know you at all.

Our friendship has been rather one-sided; we have tended to emphasize only one aspect.

But, in the long run (and I hope it will be,) we should get better acquainted . . .

Right now, I crave, covet, and desire your companionship more than almost anything, even my work.

Today, thinking back, seeing us and how we are together, I know we are a little bit crazy, but . . . we have something very special, something unusual, very great, ... so very nice, warm and good for us both. It makes us happy, we feel good together . . .
I probably will call you tonight just for a minute.
To hear your voice and say "hello—I-love-you."
I see your smile. I touch your hand.

P—Monday, 1/20

Hi, Love!

I was just thinking after I refilled my car's gas tank, I sure wish I had a car like yours (Gremlin) instead of my gas guzzler (Matador)—the dumb thing takes $9 worth of gas for that lovely trip. Remember how we decided that it would be more feasible for me to come there? Right now, your time is more precious than mine. I can often bring my work with me or postpone it somewhat, but you usually can't. But in a couple of years, we'll renegotiate about the time. (smile) That sounds nice—I like to think about us "in a couple of years"—who knows?

Thought about you several times at school today. Such happy feelings you give me when you're in my mind! It's a good way to live and work, to be especially happy, isn't it?

I had a little trouble deciphering the first letter in your handwriting—but have had NO problems ever since. Are you writing better, or do I just know you better? Maybe both?

Oh, you dear one! You just called, and I love you bunches!

ML—Tuesday, 1/21

My birthday card is very funny, very appropriate. I really laughed and laughed. My smile turned to tears of joy when I found and read your beautiful note . . . Such a lovely note, my dear one, so welcome.

Do you realize that it was just one month ago today that . . . ? So much has happened since then, I think we have set something of a record, don't you agree? Your fault. You are very bold!
Also shameless. And nice, and sexy, and beautiful!

My heart is with you, wishing to see you and be near.

Always

P—Wednesday, 1/22 (at work)

Hi, Dear!

I'm glad you liked the note(s) in the "luggage." I enjoyed writing them—took a fairly long time, getting my thoughts put down exactly as I meant them.

Hey, I hope you'll forgive me—and trust me—I just can't burn your letters. I still re-read the early ones, as well as the more recent ones. Maybe in a year or two, ok?

I think it's sweet, what you're doing with my note—I'm pleased that you're sentimental. (Me, too.)

Lordy, Lordy, but you make me happy! Sometime I'll tell you about how my feelings for (and about) you have changed, modified, and grown. You're no more surprised (or pleased) at our rapid progress than I am. You're beginning to be with me the first thing in the morning, now. I'm starting to wake up thinking of you—such a glorious way to begin a day!

See you soon, my Love

ML—Sunday, 1/26

The time with you was unbelievably beautiful-brief.

The parting too soon, always too soon.

Believe me when I say that I am thankful beyond expression for your love, your friendship.

Sharing some time, and happines—

You are fun to be with. I laugh with you and cherish the joy of just being together.

Be secure that you are loved.

Sincerely

P.S. It is not enough to say I miss you. It is a longing, I'm sure. Ever have a longing before?

[The next letter refers to one of many times we both drove our cars on the highway to our mutual destination, with me following her.
Whenever we came to a stop sign or a stoplight, we each held up one hand, palm out, in our windshield—our way of signaling "Hi, I love you" or "Bye Honey, I'll miss you."]

P—Sunday, 1/26

Hi, Sweet Love!

Just got home—well, you may have been right—your way was almost 5 minutes shorter than mine.

The movie "Charly" is on the TV now. Did you see it, and/or read the book, Flowers for Algernon? I wept—really sobbed—when I read the end of the book. I was just thinking, I'd like to share some movies, etc. with you. Let's still think in terms of our going to a concert or play or program or something down there, ok?

Love you, Dearest!!

ML—Tuesday, 1/28

Sweetheart—

Please ignore my other letter . . . I sometimes get moments of doubt, it is hard not to.

I think I am concerned about the intensity of our feelings, so afraid it will burn itself out. If we could keep it all a little more low-key, hold back, wait, and just let things (good) happen.

Be patient with me, my doubting, my fears.

Can I, do I dare express them? You will not despair and leave me, will you? I have a fear, my own love, my sweet Pat, that the bubble will burst, the flame will die, and you will go away to a more secure, more predictable, more accessible support. This has happened to me already, before. I guess I am afraid it will happen again.

I keep thinking, "better not jump in, climbing out is so terribly difficult and painful."

In twenty-five minutes, I am going to call you. And tell you that I love you, that I miss your smile, your cheerful idiocy, your delightful (if exasperating) playfulness. You are a joyful partner, my own secret lover. I cannot get over how zonked we are.

Saw my friend Dexter. His place is ours each and every Friday . . . He says the shower is large enough for two. The devil!

P—Tuesday, 1/28 (10:30 pm)

Hi, Lover!

It's raining right now—the sound of it reminds me of our first night, when I said, "Now, it's complete." The sound of the rain outside was pleasant, but to listen to it at night while lying in your arms —or with you in my arms—was absolutely perfect! I like remembering that night—I like to remember all of our times together. So many beautiful moments already! So much happiness! Sometimes I get overwhelmed, thinking of the future possibilities.

I'm concerned that we find the right balance between an awareness of reality and the greatest possible joy. I hate to see us enjoy our happiness less because we're wondering how real it is, or how long it will last, or what if . . . ?

Stolen days or moments may be our lot right now, but not so much in a few months, maybe? I'm already tentatively planning it. When the time comes, will you see about my getting a room there? Hope I can. All my love

and devotion

P—Sunday, 2/2

Hi again, Sweet!

I've decided to send you this first card early—it's been 15 years since I've seen a card with this particular message. Wasn't it just last week that I told you about buying one like it when I was in college? (. . . in 1959 or 1960!)

The card's message on the outside was:

"I REALLY LIKE YOU!"

and on the inside:

> *"I Love a Rainy Night!"*

"I LIKE YOU BETTER'N CHUNKLIT—CUBBERED GRAB CRACKERS!"

(. . . and I REALLY like chunklit-cubbered grab crackers!)

[My humor had not matured in the past fifteen years.]

ML—Monday, 2/3

If we can cool it and not get upset or blow it somehow, I think that eventually we can arrange some very neat times. Like this summer. Whereas, this part: frantic, head-over-heels goofy— is wonderful, I am looking forward to the more peaceful times you mentioned. Do you suppose we will eventually calm down?

My love, always

P—Monday, 2/3 (noon)

Hi, Honey!

Wanted to write right away, to let you know

things look better today. (I still miss you, but it hurts a little less.) (The patient will live.) (grin)

I gave out the contest medals today—he choir was pretty "up in the air"—we had a good time. I told them we'd have to get right down to hard work tomorrow—start getting ready for the whole choir's contest. (We have less than 2 months.) I think they should do well this year. (Good spirit, co-operative-ness, some good talent, etc.) Onward and upward, as they say.

ML—Tuesday, 2/4

My dear love,

Your letters are overpowering . Thrilling, full of your excitement and love . . .

I am just a person who cares for you very much —the same and yet different from the one you observed with such hesitant suspicion not so many weeks ago. Remember?

Your call early this morning was loving and thoughtful . . .

Very, very great to hear your voice. I must think more about this weekend . . . It will be certainly a trial run to see if we can work together. If we fail to function it could be serious.

Dear One, Pat. I am very much in earnest about us controlling . . . This is our first big challenge together.

Then, she wrote out all of the words to one of our favorite songs, "You're My Home" (Helen Reddy)

P—Tuesday, 2/4

Hi, Love!

You talked about putting your heart down on paper. I've felt the same way, Honey. We both have

to have a lot of trust for each other to put our innermost thoughts and feelings down on paper the way we have; we both have a lot to lose. I do thank you though, for not pressing the idea of a "bi-weekly burning session"—I still go back over some of your earliest letters—still love them just as much the forty-ninth time as I did the first time I read them! (No, I didn't really count how many times I'd re-read them!)

My love, always . . .

ML—Tuesday, 2/11

Dear One,

You know, your letters are so good, so like you. When I read them, I can see your eyes smiling, sparkling, like you usually are. Sometimes when we are together, and especially when you think I am not watching, you get a very serious and sad look on your face, like you used to have . . . What are you thinking at those times, my dear one, that makes you so sad?

Be happy, be secure, you are loved. We grow closer each week, more perfectly true friends as we already are lovers.

I love you, think of you many times each day.
Yours

[I'm not sure where the rest of my letters to her are — hers are better, anyway.]

Sunday, 2/16 (evening)

The time with you was beautiful, hope you think so too. I think I like you best when you are serious and pseudo-business-like; all the time there is this feeling that comes through (at least it seems this way to me) . . . an undercurrent of suppressed mischievousness . . . delightful and impish. A natural effervescence that is about to be let loose, or wants to be let loose. Your CHILD. Your child needs to play, unrestrained by years and years of moralistic taboos . . . You are lovely and good, a delight and a joy.

My dear one, you are the best medicine for me. We will see each other soon, the time will fly . . . I love you very much, but if I did not, I would still value your friendship, and admire your wit and talent.

Thursday, March 6
[Written in Pat's apartment, while she's at work, across the street]

Dear Love:

Thank you for the use of this typewriter. It has been a joy touching where you touch. One day, when it is necessary and appropriate, when you do some typing for me, I will know the wherewithal you do it. I have no complaints except, the blue color of this instrument could and should be more nearly the color of your eyes for greatest beauty.

It is fun to work in your apartment, except my heart skips now and then when I hear someone on the stairs.

Do not run, but walk fast.

Monday, March 10

I was so unbelievably tired today. I asked myself, "Who do you think you are?" The pace we set together would be difficult for a young person. Now I feel every muscle in my whole body . . .

It is really fun to be with you, even the danger of snow and discovery has an excitement; we are each too adventurous for our own good . . . My thoughts and my love are with you . . .

"I Never Wanted to Love a Man . . . the way that I wanta love you"	

I really, really want you for my own, myself alone. Selfishly. You are beautiful and irrepressible, you delight and charm. You utterly wear me out. I love you. More.

Wednesday, March 12
[Letter #1]
Dear Love,

I am home, sick . . . Headachy, dizzy, have had cramping and upset stomach. I need care and love and attention. Somebody to bring me broth and aspirin. Someone to put a hand on my aching muscles and whisper soft. Today I feel like a CHILD.

I went to sleep with you on my mind last night. Often I do that, but this time I was trying to figure out the what-you-might-call ramifications of us. What are we, you and I, and what are we to each other? Feeling trapped and two-faced, talking about freedom while clinging to the established security. Hoping for a solution within the "establishment," yet wanting to not, and do in a revolutionary way.

STOP
This letter is a bunch of bullship.

See letter #2.

(Still March 12)
Little Sweetheart,

Letter from you came. As usual. Your letters—like you—good and full of simple love, giving and sharing. I love you very much, Pat. You are my real delight. I sometimes wish I could stand on a hill and proclaim to one and all: "See my pretty lover, my charming and wonderful one!"

Yes, I miss you terribly also. I love you for your gentleness . . . Just now, today, I do not feel up to my work and wish to retreat from it back into your arms. But that is because I do not feel too good; tomorrow, the challenge will be met.

Whatever else we are, we care about each other. We enjoy each other, our companionship is mutually enjoyable.

The thought of our continuing joy together is like a tonic.

"You are a child of the universe . . ."

Whatever else, little sweetheart, let us hold on to this treasure between us.

Thursday, 3/13
Dear Love,

Went to see Frank, (her counselor at Ball State) he helps me a lot, just to talk to. We discussed you; he says my face lights up when I start talking about you. Hmmm. It shows . . . He sees our relationship as all positive . . . I love you dearly.

(Later)

Just talked with you. You sounded so good. Very sure, stable.

Looking back, thinking about our insecurity at the start, seeing us now, much more at ease and relaxed with each other. It's good. It's just so very good. We are right for each other, supportive at the right times and hopefully will continue being that way.

Your love is like a warm cloak. When wrapped in

it, there is a calmness and serenity. That is another part, besides the excitement

Yours

Monday, 3/17
Very dearest one—

I try to look at things objectively, especially when we are apart , but it is very hard. Dexter says (and he was referring to getting married) "Hell, I might die tomorrow, might as well enjoy and be happy." I told him I felt much the same way. He knew what I was referring to.

Sweetheart, my love, always. Always. I love you. Sometimes it scares me, though. But . . .
Hell, I might die tomorrow . . .

You are lovely, I trust your judgment, be happy. You are loved.

Wednesday, 3/19

To my very patient and understanding Lover,
You are kind and tolerant of my oscillating confidence.

Your voice and manner are quiet
and soothing when most needed.

We are equally eager together and
we are disappointed about the same things, usually.

In the short, yes often frantic, time we have known each other

We have established a rare union.
So sweet,so good. Beautiful.
We will keep this between us, for us, as long as we can.

I appreciate your joyous and spontaneous humor.

Your sparkle. It is my happiness.
You are my love and delight.
Your touch never fails to set me alive.

Without you there is a tolerable loneliness
With you, my living is unspeakably more than it ever was before.

Don't change. Never leave.

[I believe the next letter was written after Mary Lee's young adult children had become aware of my existence—and they were NOT happy about me!

I believe they felt that I was someone who was "taking advantage" of their Mother. I remember the look of utter disgust on Joe's face, and later, Jan's, on two separate occasions when each saw me with her.

Mary Lee wanted them to meet me, but when Jannie saw us together in the Student Union, she turned and went back out the door. The time Joe had seen us he walked away, after directing a withering stare at me.

It took some time, but we eventually got to know one another and became loving friends and family. At this time, though, Mary Lee was feeling incredibly torn between losing them or me, because it seemed to be an insurmountable situation.]

Monday, 3/24

Today it is very hard to focus my attention and get on with the work here. My nerves are really a wreck. Suddenly, after all these months, I really feel that things are about to go to pieces . . .

I will always remember Saturday and us at Todd and Jan's—how upset I was and desperate. When I advised you to get the hell out of my life and the confused mess going on, you said "No, I won't go." Perhaps you didn't realize I heard you, how clearly I heard you and how wonderful and hopeful it made me feel. I am so afraid, inside, that I will lose or alienate your love which I treasure and am so grateful for. You are dear and fine and so deserving of a stable, above-board companion. How can it be wise for us to continue? Yet, with all my heart, this is what I want . . .

You are my dear and lovely sweetheart and what we have had already cannot be forgotten. Let's hope it is merely a prelude to the future.
Sincerely—

Tuesday, 3/25 (7:00 am)

Dear One—I guess the pace is telling. This morning the getting up has been rough. Thought about you while trying to sleep. There are many things which worry me. My concern is for you—your stability and happiness. Also for mine. I have been fighting a feeling which is telling me to be cautious, careful. Retreat, even. I have the feeling that I may be complicating your life. I care for you—want you to be happy. I want to be happy, too. I wonder, my dear love. Can we both handle it? Think carefully.
With love

Thursday, 3/27

Mind is in a turmoil. Thoughts of many kinds, mixed up, pretty much mixed up.

The wide-spread concept of this person being all-powerful, strong is greatly over-stated. Feel very alone today . . . Hardly know what to do about "finishing out my life."

Did not expect the rejection that am getting . . . very deep hurt for her somehow.

Be patient and know I love you. That you love me too is amazing and marvelous.

Friday, 3/28

Have been feeling depressed and greatly in need. Just before sleep I read your letters and the book you bought. Really feel like a mis-fit, lonely. Surely you and I share a bond of identity that is unique but very real. You are important to me. I dearly love you.

Monday, April 7

Dear Pat,

I am so sorry. Somehow my own inadequacies of acceptance have been imposed upon you and this is unfair. Be kind to yourself and love yourself, for you are the person I love very much. And I will try not to hurt you anymore.

Let us both work hard and do what we have to do.

Be happy knowing that I care for you no matter what.

Tuesday, April 8

LOVE LETTER
Have you doubted for one moment?
Have you doubted for one second?
Sweetheart, my dear one, my love.
My one love,
Please know. I love you.
Just twenty-four hours since I
   saw the parting tear-stained face.
Oh sweet little one. Nor more tears.
I care for you. No help for it.
Whatever you are, or are not.
No matter to me somehow.

Don't go away. Stay and wait and
   be patient.
For we have much to share.
Whatever else, we will keep what
   we now have.
I want it. Do You?
Oh please stay and see what will be.

Wednesday, April 9

Dear Love,

Next time let's have dinner up the line closer to you and share the distance a bit more equally. Long summer days are almost here . . .
   As ever

Tuesday, April 15

My dearest and secret love,

A letter came today, such a great treat to get your loving and humorous notes. You and your letters are much alike, endearing and good, kind, generous, sharing

Monday, April 28

My own dear love,

It seems to me (occasionally) that you are one of the very nicest things I know about in this world; soft and smiling and full of a little bit of the devil. I like you. I really do. I forgot to kiss all the freckles on your arm. Write that down.

It is storming here, with lightning and rain. I think it would be scary in a cemetery, at least it would be if I were alone.

   Always yours

P.S. Don't be concerned for a minute about T—or anyone else, for that matter. It's you.

Wednesday, April 30

My own dear moody love—

No more tears—no more. Will you try to accept and be secure? Can't we both? Dear one, I will not desert you or leave, or withdraw my affection, or stop caring or go away. That is not saying we may each not become confused and hurt occasionally. But we can go along and take it in stride and keep on loving and caring and, of course, being patient and careful. ?

I have been sitting here looking at people. It's amazing why you sometimes criticize your own person when by comparison you are such a really nice looking thing. Really, the best of all I see. And I'm really looking. (Not really)

It's raining again. Does Dork (little brown stuffed donkey) like the rain? It was great being with you. You are my love.

Friday, May 2

To my sweet lady,
So very wonderful to be with you
And to love you—to share.
Each time the bond grows
And strengthens, we know each other
a little better, a small amount more.

My thoughts are with you many times each day.
To me,
Like a long distance vivid awareness.
Not very explainable, is it?

But something complicated inside of me reaches out
and finds and holds gratefully to you.
When you respond, it is a rare magic.
We will be.

Tuesday, May 6

Your devilishness is both exasperating and exciting; you're right, I love it, still don't know what to do with you or about you sometimes. One thing I do not seem to be able to tolerate is doing without you.

I'll still be leaving here at 5 or 5:30. Have an appointment. With a very important person. A little strange individual, but quite nice. Good hands. Other things good, too. Lips.

Feel better today. Backache some better. Saw Dexter and Janese this morning. Both beautiful.

Friday, May 9

My dear One—

Please consider getting rid of all my letters, they are just pieces of paper. Sweetheart. Do me a favor, —shred and burn them all. I will write you many, many more; but please do not keep them. I will love you even more, if you do this.

Monday, May 12

My darling, my special one—

I read my Monday letter already, I couldn't wait, but then resealed it and will read it again tomorrow. Your letters are so very, very nice to read.

It is difficult for me to express adequately my appreciation of you, your gentle consideration for me, your instant attention, kindness, good humor, smiles, joking and mischievous fun, your loving touch, forgiveness for my ambiguous abruptness, the times you give me, sympathy, generosity. Most of all, for your love, which I see in your eyes, in your every expression, and which closes around me when I doubt or am sad.

Thank you, Sweetheart.
In return, you have me.
Around your little finger

Monday, May 19

LOVE LETTER

One touch, one smile
One more together again
Each time a renewed miracle of joyous awareness
The expectation fully realized.
How can it be true that you still do care?
As I do.
Two strangers, really—but no more.
Lovers, soul mates, astonished and grateful

You make me happy beyond believing. That you exist in my life, that you allow me to love you.
Oh wow!
Don't ever stop.
Stay.
As long as possible.
I love you.

Thursday, May 22

We will be apart now for a week or so—it will be a lonely time but we can take it. As soon as I get back I will call you.

There will be the week when we cannot contact each other at all, either because of distance or circumstance. I want you to know that I will be thinking of you every hour, every day and lonely (inside) for you. Time will surely only increase our need and appreciation of each other . . .

My heart is with my sweet lover

Tuesday, June 3 (at Muncie)

My darling, my sweetheart—
It would have been great together—here, then back. I dreamed it all the way. It was raining . . .

We need to talk and touch and be close. Soon, very soon, we will be. Let's concentrate on making every day special.

Do I love you? Let me count the ways. 1,2,3,4, 5,6,7,8,9,10,11,12,13,14,18, 19, 56, 3,475, 10, 13, 4, 510, 37, 99, 101, 10, 2 million, 6, 798, 354, 81, 411, 412, 80 jillion, 450 quadrillion—infinity.

[Then, we spent the summer together at Ball State University—we had separate abodes, but she lived with me!—incredible!!!

Her next letter is at the end of the summer, when we had to be apart again, to begin the new school year.]

Thursday, August 28–9 AM

[Pat left Muncie at 6:15 am—gone back home to teach.]

Dearest—
Please write to me here, at least for a while.
I miss you already. You have endeared yourself to me in a hundred ways. No one is better to me or for me. How will I ever make it without you?

Although I may poke fun and aggravate you, even

criticize, I know the truth, which is, that you are a fine, good, and beautiful person. I love you as I have no other.

Take care of yourself and be good to yourself for me while we are apart. If you pray, beseech whatever gods that are, that we may be allowed some happiness together before it's all over. We have already had some, and that cannot be taken away.

I will miss knowing your day-to-day activities, plans, experiences.

> For now, be safe.
> Cherish us.

After living together during that first summer, we found that the ensuing separations were increasingly painful for us, until eventually, we wept each time we had to leave one another. It became more and more clear that as soon as it was possible, we needed to be together—permanently.

These letters continued on into the new school year, anytime we were separated for more than just a few days, until Mary Lee received her doctorate in May of 1978 and we were finally able to share a home together in New Haven.

Indeed, for the rest of our lives together, the letters flourished whenever we were separated for more than a week, such as during her four-month sabbatical for her continued research and publications at Ball State University; during April and May of 1991, her three- or four-week stay at her daughter Jan's California home before and after the birth of Katie, Mary Lee's third grandchild; and for a similar stay with Jannie and her family during February and March in 1995, after the birth of Julie, her fourth grandchild.

Once in the early 1980s, we tried taking separate vacations (simultaneously) with our respective families (Mary Lee in California and mine in Nevada,) but Jannie finally said to her, "Mom, next time, bring Pat with you; I'm getting tired of you moping around here because you're missing her so much!" And I found myself wishing that Mary Lee was with me to share me experiences, too. All of our trips and vacations have been together since that debacle.

Years later, when Mary Lee had passed on and I was gradually going through her things, I kept finding loving and funny cards that we had given to each other for any occasion during each year. At first, they touched me and brought me to tears of grief and loneliness for her. Now, I keep a stash of them lying out in several rooms of our home, and I enjoy reading them from time to time, and remembering.

Below is one of my favorite cards I gave to her.

What a lovely thing to do —
spend my lifetime loving you!
Planning days that bring us pleasure,
building memories two can treasure,
Reaching milestones, one by one,
sharing problems, sharing fun,
Being close — the best friends ever,
making dreams come true together.

Chapter 4
Our First Decade

January, 1975 through December, 1984

How in the world do I tell about our thirty-six years together without making each chapter sound like a "Dear Diary"? Bo-r- r- r- r-ing!

We always took a great deal of pleasure in taking pictures of our activities, of friends and family members, and of each other in various situations—over seventy large albums, filled with all these photos, plus four more smaller silver albums containing highlights of each decade, which we keep on display on the buffet table in the living room.

Maybe looking through all of these albums would be a good way to jog my memory, so I can tell about some important ways that our relationship began, grew, developed, and changed over the years.

THE GOOD

January 9, 1975—I made the decision (it wasn't difficult) to make the drive to Muncie, Indiana for the first time to be with Mary Lee. Neither of us knew what the future held for us, but both of us already felt a strong magnetic pull to be together, which never abated. I arrived Thursday night and stayed through Sunday. Later, it became a pattern that I would arrive on any day after I had finished teaching for the week, or any day that school was cancelled because of the numerous snow storms we had during a couple of winters, because I always kept a packed bag in the

back of my car. For maximum time together, I would not leave her place until six a.m. on Mondays to make the drive back to school, walk in, and be ready to teach that morning.

Every morning we were together, no matter where

| "You're My Home" |

we were, I would wake up with a huge grin on my face as I gazed over at her—which she returned, as soon as she was also awake. She was correct in one of her early letters to me, when she predicted that we would laugh a lot together. One of the first challenges we had was just to be able to fall asleep at night, because we were always so excited and happy to be together. It took quite a while, but we were finally able to adjust . . . and sleep.

I remember telling Mary Lee more than once, that whenever we shared a meal, the food tasted better. As a matter of fact, everything that we shared or did together was always better, and continued to be, for all those years to follow.

In the Ball State University biology lab, I would sit on a stool, watching Mary Lee do her research procedures and experiments, not understanding most of it, but willing to learn and looking for ways I might be helpful to her. I noticed that I could barely read the labels she was printing on the caps of the many scintillation vials she was using, so I volunteered to label them for her from then on. Her sometimes illegible handwriting in her letters to me had already become a joke between us, and we both agreed that my printing was neater than hers. Thus, I became her lab assistant.

She always wore a white lab coat (and usually, a white turtleneck sweater underneath it) when doing her lengthy research procedures in that lab. I realized years later that I still adored seeing her wear her lab coat while she worked in the lapidary room of our home, cutting, forming, and polishing the stones she was preparing for her jewelry creations. The white turtleneck still makes me remember that's how she looked when I fell in love with her, and I would get somewhat giddy when she wore it.

Our first photos together were taken in a small photo booth at the Muncie Mall. For years, the last two of those four small photos were hidden away in the bottom of my nightstand drawer; now they're in this book, for God and everyone to see! About time, don'cha think?

Labeling scintillation vials

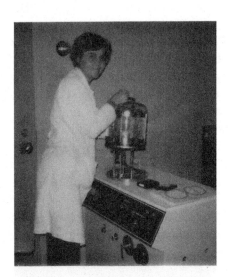

Carbon coating

1975-We begin!

Mary Lee introduced me to feminism, through the National Organization for Women (N.O.W.) chapter in Muncie. Sue Errington was the president of the chapter at that time, and she became a life-long friend of both of us during the ensuing years. In later years, every time Sue ran for a political office, we made donations to her campaign; she was an Indiana State Senator, and as I write this, she was recently elected to the Indiana legislature as a State Representative. Sue continues to be one of those highly intelligent but un-assuming women, dedicated to serving her constitu-ents, exceptionally well-informed, and also "willing and able to work across the aisle" kind of women who are increasingly bringing a new and inspiring level of ethics and positive action into our governments. I'm still your fan, Sue!

During the summer of 1975, I took several elec-tronic music courses at the Ball State University music school, living just one block away from Mary Lee's rooming house. She spent most of that summer living with me in the house I was renting. She cooked for us, and introduced me to fried okra, a food popular in Henryetta, Oklahoma, the small town where she was born and lived for years. For those brief weeks, we had our own place.

For much of that first year, we stayed in the "W" Motel almost every week. I remember one evening, she apologized to me that we didn't have a nicer place to be together. I replied that it didn't matter to me where we were—only that we were together. Wherever we're together, you're my home . . . became a very important truism for us.

Sometime later, Dexter Canada, one of Mary Lee's friends, told her that he wanted to meet me in person. Then he offered his second floor apartment for us to meet and stay whenever I was in town, and he would stay with his girlfriend, Janese.

Pat and Sue Errington

Dexter and Janese at their wedding

It was small, but clean and private and gener-ously donated to us for our use. Many times we would talk through most of the night. I remember one night that I told her, "I'm so incredibly happy when I'm with you; I wish I could spend the rest of my life with you." She replied that she couldn't imagine that ever happen-ing for anyone like us. She had never heard of it, of permanent relationships for others like us. But it was a wonderful dream to have.

> *"It's Too Late to Turn Back Now... I Believe, I Believe, I Believe I'm Falling in Love"*

In September, 1976, Mary Lee moved into a trailer on the edge of the city. Her landlady and family lived on the other side of the lot. They had a young boy, who had that Muncie southern drawl and had difficulty saying our names. He called us Murdy Lay and Payut. We laughed about it, and years later were calling each other by those names, and writing it on our Christmas gift tags to each other. We also celebrated our first Christmas together in that trailer.

That summer, we planted beautiful flowers around the front of our third home together and even painted our names on the mailbox by the road.

Winter, 1977—Right outside of the front door of our trailer, Pat made, *not* a snowman, but a snow tit on the ground. Mary Lee was mortified by it, especially after I named what it was.

Uh—Why is there no picture of it? Read on . . .

I need to share some interesting background about the previous picture, and the turmoil it has recently brought to Mary Lee and me as we were creating this chapter.

I had scanned the original photo, then copied and pasted it where you would have seen it. Then more recently, I had reason to copy and paste it into another form of the book—but it wouldn't come up when I attempted to paste it . . . and then suddenly, it disappeared from the other page where it had been for weeks. I couldn't get it to show up in either version of that page. Late into the night, I worked on it for over an hour, when, frustrated, weary, and discouraged, I finally gave up and went to bed, wondering why it suddenly wouldn't work.

I even wondered if Mary Lee had caused the problem, since it was caused by something electrical with the computer, and I've learned that spirits are electrical, just like we are: our brains, our circulatory system, our nervous system, our heart, etc. If she did it, I was angry with her. I determined that I would ask Mary Lee about it during my next session with Tina Zion (a very gifted fourth generation psychic).

When I showed Tina the photo, she laughed, and Mary Lee was already in the process of telling Tina about it, saying that indeed, she didn't want it in the book!

I said that the picture was *not* a reflection about Mary Lee, but rather, it revealed something about *my* personality, the mischievous, sometimes outrageous part of me, who liked to push the boundaries with my actions. I said that in the previous chapter of our letters to each other, Mary Lee had mentioned several times about my playful and sometimes mischievous humor. In chapter 3, in her February 16th letter to me, she referred to it as letting my inner child out to play, after having experienced a more repressed childhood.

At this point, Tina laughed and said that we would have to discuss it and work it out between us. Mary Lee eventually relented and said, "Okay, the photo can be in the book." Two days later, when I later opened to that page, the photo suddenly reappeared by itself! With the help of Mary Lee.

However, the next evening, it disappeared again, and I expressed my anger to her, saying I didn't want to write the book with her, if she was going to fight me or sabotage me. I shut down the computer and spent the rest of the evening angrily doing some emotional eating. When I finally went into our semi-darkened bedroom and approached the bedside lamp, I dejectedly said to her, "I know you won't be flashing 'I love you' to me tonight." She immediately flashed the lamp before I had even touched it. I cried, and she flashed it again. My anger melted away. It seemed to be our first fight from different dimensions!

I awoke the next morning, wondering if she needed me to explore the significance of that picture and my sometimes adolescent humor. So I began writing about it . . .

I realized that very early in our relationship, my personality had begun to change noticeably. With the unconditional love she expressed toward me, and the unmitigated joy she felt with me, it was as if a very negative part of me from my past was now gone: the self-hatred, the depression, and moodiness, the fear and discouragement about the lonely future I had long presumed was in store for me.

I now had the assurance that she would laugh at my silly jokes, she would take seriously the feelings, opinions, and ideas that I now felt free to express, and that she would accept me for who I really was.

By the way, I'm crying as I write this.

This was pretty heady stuff, for one who had previously never felt acceptable, who seemed to be the odd one of the family who never seemed to fit in, who always felt separate and lonely. So, I began to think and act in ways that would be normal . . . uh . . . for a junior high type mentality . . . a bit inappropriate, sometimes even shocking, and glorying in it, just like

> *"Because I Knew You, I Have Been Changed for Good"*
> *"Georgy Girl"* (. . . *there's another Georgy deep inside* . . .)

a few of my junior high age students sometimes acted, especially with someone they really liked . . . trying to be noticed by the object of their affection or respect, even if it was sometimes over the top.

Back in the next session with Tina and Mary Lee, Tina informed me that when she was driving there in her car, Mary Lee was there with her! She'd never done that before. She told Tina she was worried about me, and she wanted to get there and make things right between us! I read aloud to both of them what I'd just written, about the reasons I acted as I sometimes did. When I finished reading it, I found that Mary Lee still didn't want that picture in our book.

Looking back on the previous session, I remembered that her okay had been somewhat reluctant at the time, but I hadn't noticed that. Now, I told her that I had already decided that very morning, that it didn't matter that much to me, and if she really wanted it out, it would not appear in the book.

Her response was, "That's a good compromise," and we all three relaxed.

I guess it's easier now to see why, the longer Mary Lee and I were together all those years, interacting in a most positive, loving, and accepting way, I would so often proclaim to others the words that would become the title of this book: "I came alive in '75!"

Back in 1974, music and food were my main friends, my only joy.

The first two winters, I drove through many heavy snowstorms to be with her, safe and warm in that trailer. Once, on Interstate Highway 69, I drove for many miles on a very narrow path with twelve-foot-high walls of solid snow on either side. As I drove, they kept announcing on the radio that anyone who got stuck driving in that snowstorm would be arrested, because it had been declared a snow emergency, and no one was to be driving in it.

I didn't tell Mary Lee that I was on my way there, because I didn't want her to be worried about me. I just showed up, and plowed my car into the large bank of snow in front of her trailer. What a great relief to arrive, and what a stunned but joyful welcome I received! By the way, thank you, God, for all the protection you provided me during my more foolhardy stunts like that one!

During the next year or so, we became very familiar with many of the Bee Gee's and Donna Summer's songs, as we energetically took up . . . disco dancing! Good exercise, great social activity, and fun! I remembered telling her early on that I had never known anyone who could dance while they were sitting down in a chair, at a table! She loved to dance!

We loved some things about that old trailer. We spent many rainy nights listening to the rain on it's metal roof, as we drifted into a happy, peaceful sleep as we held each other in the night. Also, we sometimes enjoyed listening to the individual train whistles as they passed by in the distance.

Summer, 1977—We planted & harvested a good-sized vegetable garden behind the trailer, ate healthy meals, and regularly rode our bikes several miles up and down the country hills. Once, I was the lookout while Mary Lee filched a couple of tasty ears of corn from one of the fields we passed—guilty pleasures, but we still enjoyed eating them for supper that evening.

I remember that Mary Lee's grown son and daughter had exhibited very negative feelings about me when they each unexpectedly saw me with her for the first time that summer. They both loved their mom, and I believed that they sought to protect her from the likes of me. Joe had looked fiercely at me and didn't speak to me as I sat in the car, and I was sure he probably felt as if I had seduced his mother and was not someone who was a good influence in her life. By the way, I just recently learned that some of the members of my family had also felt the same way about Mary Lee, at first—until they got to know her.

Some days later, Mary Lee's daughter Jan was just coming into the entrance of the Ball State Student Union where we were eating, and Mary Lee got up and went over to Jan, wanting her to meet me. I remember the disgusted look on Jan's face as she immediately spun around and went back out the door. Mary Lee dearly loved her kids, and wanted very much for them to get to know me and to have a positive relationship with me. It didn't look promising . . .

Later that summer, Mary Lee persuaded Jan to go with both of us to the Delaware County Fair, held in Muncie. It was an uncomfortable and strained time. We went up to a booth (where I believe we were supposed to throw balls into baskets,) and the barker kept saying, "You can't lose—I guarantee that you'll win a prize here!" He kept cajoling us to keep paying and playing for a prize that he promised us, when suddenly, he said, "Nope, you didn't make it; no prize for you." We were mystified and feeling swindled and angry, but powerless. I purposefully strode away without saying a word to either of them.

Soon, I returned with a police officer and told him how the man had promised us over and over that we would win a prize. The officer asked if that was true, and both Mary Lee and Jannie confirmed what I was saying. Then he told the guy that if he didn't want to be shut down, he had to give us a prize—any one that we picked out. The man was *not* happy at hearing that. I looked over all of the booth's prizes carefully, and chose the largest, most expensive one hanging there—a large stuffed, brown-and-tan buffalo. He reluctantly took it down and gave it to me, and I promptly gave it to Jannie. She was quite astonished, and I felt like it was the beginning of a beautiful friendship. Her attitude and manner toward me softened during and after that misadventure, and she began to see me in a different light. I had felt very protective of both her and her mother and had acted on it.

By the way, we called our prize Buffy, and a year later, we gave him to my nephew, Brian, who was young and moving far away to Nevada with his family.

Starting sometime in 1976 or '77, we were missing each other so much that we began also meeting every Tuesday for supper together at a little restaurant just off the highway near Gas City. The distance was about halfway for each of us to drive. That little eating

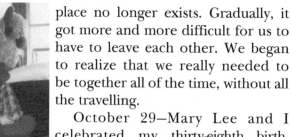

Christmas, 1977
Mary Lee, Jan, and Joe

Christmas, 1977, Pat, Jan, and Joe

place no longer exists. Gradually, it got more and more difficult for us to have to leave each other. We began to realize that we really needed to be together all of the time, without all the travelling.

October 29—Mary Lee and I celebrated my thirty-eighth birthday in her trailer, where my "Murdy" cooked a wonderful meal, and she had also baked and decorated a birthday cake for the occasion.

Two months later, I became more a part of Mary Lee's family, when Joe, Jan, Mary Lee, and I all celebrated the 1977 Christmas in my new home in New Haven, Indiana. I had moved out of my small apartment and into my first real home, just one week before Christmas. Not much furniture yet, but definitely a friendly, fun time for all four of us. From the time they were tiny children, Jan and Joe always had the sweetest, most loving, supportive—and fun relationship, and now I had become a part of it.

April, 1978—Mary Lee studied diligently and passed her doctoral orals—we all celebrate at her trailer.

May 20, 1978—Graduation: Mary Lee is awarded her doctorate at the ceremony. I couldn't see where he was standing or sitting, but I remember hearing Joe's voice calling out, "Way to go, Mom!" as she received her degree. We all shared some really good pizza afterwards.

After we moved Dr. Richeson out of the Muncie trailer and into our New Haven home, we had a housewarming party for our friends, family, and new neighbors; took our first vacation together in Gatlinburg, Tennessee; visited with both of our families; caulked and painted the outside of the windows of our new home; shopped for fun at a giant flea market in Shipshewana, Indiana; began planting flowers along the borders of our large back yard; then, we got some family and friends together to help us build a privacy fence around our back yard, and then took part in our first ten-mile walkathon for the ERA! ! (The Equal Rights Amendment)

Soon, one room at a time, we began to make the house our own, painting the walls and ceiling, having a good quality padding and carpeting professionally installed, and buying a few things to make the room ours. We took our time, paying for each part of the project before going on to the next room. This became a pattern for us throughout the ensuing years: DON'T GO INTO DEBT!

This philosophy served us very well. Both of us saved regularly; then, when we wanted to do something that might be expensive for us (a vacation or project) we paid for it up front—or within thirty days, if it was going on a credit card. Years later, we were mystified and feeling slightly insulted, when a credit card salesman referred to us as freeloaders because we never paid a penny of interest to them.

"We've Only Just Begun"

THE BAD—AND THE UGLY

For about a year and a half, we were incredibly, head-over-heels happy. But we were also very naïve and trusting. We met someone the summer of 1976 and looked forward to a new friendship. It happened very slowly and gradually and took both of us by surprise. This new friend turned out to be an interloper into our relationship, and Mary Lee was drawn into it before she realized exactly what was happening. She was being courted and eventually seduced. She spent much of that summer singing the songs, "Torn Between Two Lovers" and "My Heart Belongs to Me." Every time she sang them, my heart was wrenched a little more. I will refer to "The Inter-Loper simply as "TIL" from now on. TIL professed to having two rules, and broke them both: "Don't mess with married women" and "Don't break into committed couples."

"You Don't Bring Me Flowers . . . anymore"

When I finally realized what had been happening while Mary Lee and I were living in different cities, and how far it had already gone, the boundless joy we once felt had deteriorated into a tormented, painful time for both of us. Mary Lee at one point expressed to me, "I've spent my whole adult life as a dutiful wife and mother; now I want to explore different options. Life is too short; I want it all, and I want it now."

"Tell Her . . . You Belong to Me"

As time went on, I discovered I developed a fury inside me that shocked and frightened me, as it became expressed over and over. TIL was jeopardizing and robbing me of the most incredible love, joy, and hope of my life, of my . . . our future, and I lashed out in jealousy, fear, rage, and a deep sense of loss I had never, ever known before!

I yelled at TIL on the phone from the empty trailer. I drove out into the country and spied on them with my binoculars from across the road. I felt powerless to stop what was happening, and I asked myself over and over, "What am I doing? This is not me; this is *not* who or what I am!" I was acting like a wild animal that had turned vicious when a loved one was threatened by an outside force. Then, Mary Lee began to discourage me from driving down to visit her in Muncie. She said she needed her space, and wanted to have no outside pressure from either of us to try to persuade her or convince her.

At one point, when she had to come to Fort Wayne for a doctor's appointment (which I had always driven her to and then taken her to my place to help heal the physical pain from those treatments she endured,) I told her I would not be meeting her when she came to Fort Wayne this time; I couldn't abide the situation any longer. To both of us, it sounded like I was breaking up with her, and I guess I was.

When she arrived at the doctor's office and got out of her car, she looked around for me; I had parked almost a block away and watched her from inside my car, where she couldn't see me. It hurt me to see the morose look of disappointment and sadness on her face as she turned to go into the building. I still loved her so much that I needed to catch a glimpse of her, but the pain on her face magnified my own pain as I watched her go inside alone.

Later, at my school, as I sat with some of the other teachers during my preparation period and during lunch, I couldn't enter into the conversations; I couldn't talk, because I was continually on the verge of tears. I began to realize the depth of the depression I was sinking into, which continued to grow for days and days. My heart was broken for the loss of what might have been. I was inconsolable, but I held it all in. I didn't know how I could survive without her in my life. Sometimes people say, "It's better to have loved and lost, than never to have loved at all." Wrong!

The hell of this situation continued for almost two years, whether we were in separate cities or together in Muncie, or even later, when we began living together in my new home in New Haven.

THE HEALING BEGINS

During that tortuous summer in Muncie, we were both getting regular counselling by separate members of the psychology staff at Ball State. One time, when we were extremely angry at each other and unable to deal with it, we asked for a joint counseling session with both of them present. We sat a few feet away from each other, like two fierce bulldogs, with both of our counselors sitting across the room from us, listening and observing. We were still quite angry with each other, speaking in accusatory tones. Suddenly, I angrily blurted out something to her that was harsh and mean, causing her to break down crying, and I immediately sought to comfort her.

"Lance the Boil"

A few minutes later, our counselors asked us if we were aware of how my posture, facial expression, and tone of voice had suddenly been transformed as Mary Lee burst into tears and expressed her pain. It was quite a rapid metamorphosis in me, as my love and concern had immediately dissipated any anger I'd been feeling, as I went over to her side emotionally. They had been noticing both of us doing this during the sometimes heated session, without either of us being aware of it, and they called it to our attention.

They taught us about the strong bond of love that was at the core of both of our beings, no matter how rough the situation became. This lesson didn't immediately clear up the present situation, but it gave us a very powerful tool to work with for the rest of our lives together. No matter how hard headed we could sometimes be, we continued to be aware that we have this powerful cord of love that binds us together, and it makes us want only the best for one another

The final, defining moment of decision came the summer of 1978, when we'd been living together in our home in New Haven for several months. On several occasions, TIL had called at about six a.m. on the phone (which was on my side of the bed) and would ask to speak to Mary Lee. I reluctantly handed the phone to her and listened to her accept an invitation to come and spend the day with TIL at the Salamonie Reservoir—or this time, to meet at a shopping center in Fort Wayne so they could drive to Muncie together and attend a party at the home of mutual friends later that evening. At about six or seven p.m., Mary Lee called me to say that I was invited to the party, too—but that it wouldn't start until nine that night. She asked if I would drive to that Fort Wayne shopping mall and drive her car down there for her.

I replied, "Go get your own damn car! Don't expect me to help you with it!" and I angrily slammed the phone down. I had been working in the yard that day and was all hot and sweaty. I had planned to shower and change clothes for the party, when I suddenly became convinced that TIL had lied to Mary Lee about the time of the party, so they would have more time together, without my presence. I grabbed my hanger of clothes and tossed them into my car, figuring I could shower after I arrived at our friends' home for the party.

I was full of fury at the whole situation, as I drove through a small town named Markle and then barreled down the road toward the highway. By the time I reached Interstate 69, I was going ninety mph. Very shortly, I saw the flashing lights of the state trooper's unmarked car coming up behind me. I pulled over, shaking and in tears. When he asked me what was the rush, I continued to cry and said that

I'd just found out that a very dear friend of mine was seriously ill in Muncie, and I was trying to get to her. Which, in my mind, was literally true—Mary Lee was seriously ill. He handed me the speeding ticket as he cautioned me to slow down and get there safely. I was pretty sure he had probably called ahead to another officer to be on the lookout for my car, to make sure I wasn't speeding again.

It took a long time for me to reach our friends' home for the party, and I grabbed my change of clothes, still planning to ask our friends to borrow their shower so I could be more presentable. I strode in past TIL and Mary Lee. TIL smiled (smirked?) at me and said, "Hi, Pat." I angrily looked her straight in the eye and spat out, "Eat shit!!" By the way, that language was highly uncharacteristic of me—really.

As my anger flared, I spun around and stalked back out the front door, still carrying my hanger of clothes. Mary Lee immediately ran after me, calling out my name, and we both got into my car. We sat out there for a long time, talking emotionally and sometimes fiercely.

I kept crying out over and over, "You have to choose! You want to have two mutually exclusive things. You can't have it both ways. I can't take this anymore. You have to *choose*! Now—right now!" It was the nearest I've ever been to being downright hysterical. She tried to soothe me and kept agreeing with me, saying to me, "I know. You're right. I know." Finally, with both of us exhausted and somewhat calmer, she asked me if she could drive us to a motel, so that we could be alone together. She said that we needed to talk. I agreed. That night, my Murdy quietly and firmly made her choice—to stop being in a relationship with TIL. We held each other for a long time and finally slept soundly—and peacefully.

The valuable lessons we learned that night were: to continue to make new friends, but also to be less naïve, and to have a new, more realistic awareness that our wonderful, joyful, loving relationship was *not*

necessarily impervious to outside forces (or people) and that we needed to carefully guard the gift of our love and oneness, to really cherish each other and our relationship. Serious growth period here!

The next week, we drove together to the courthouse in Markle, Indiana, where I pled guilty to the charge of speeding, and I paid my fine.

Years later, when we occasionally had a joint counseling session with Laurie Rainey Schmidt, she reminded us more than once that no matter how angry or hurt we might be, we both had this strong core of love that was always there. She said that the relationships of many other couples who went through what we had endured didn't survive it. Ours did, and we emerged from the experience with a stronger and more mature relationship.

In the early 1980s Mary Lee and I were each elected President of the Northeast Indiana N.O.W. chapter, and we built it into a very large and active chapter in the Fort Wayne area. We were a couple of those pioneer activists of the '70s and '80s, sometimes reaching out as far as Illinois and Oklahoma, being part of a movement that literally changed history and the lives of many girls, young women, older women—and men and boys, too.

We continued to feel a surge of pride each time a woman broke another glass ceiling in literally every area of life . . . including the one who will become the first woman President of the United States!

As I looked through three large albums of photos showing our activities from the late '70s to the end of 1984, I was astounded at the dizzying array and the remarkable range of activities we shared.

A New Year's Eve party with some of my family, including lots of silliness and disco dancing in our living room and also out on the driveway; building a snowwoman in our front yard; a trip to visit Jannie in California: the beach and Disneyland; many N.O.W. (National Organization for Women) activities, including: several ERA walkathons, state and national conventions, meeting Ellie Smeal, for many years the national N.O.W. president, and meeting Betty Friedan, one of the early pioneers of feminism.

Joe and his new wife Karen took part with our N.O.W. chapter in an ERA march in a neighboring state; when Mary Lee and I were each elected president of the local chapter of N.O.W., for three years, we each gave numerous radio and TV interviews which that position entailed; our strong and large local chapter often demonstrated against sexism and we helped to build a very active coalition of feminist organizations in the Fort Wayne area.

In addition, Joe and Jan were each married during this period; Mary Lee spent many, many hours creating a little Dutch girl quilt for each of their weddings.

We also enlarged our home in 1980, adding on a garage and a large family room, in which Joe did all the wiring and we did all the finishing of the inside, painting, staining, sawing, and putting up the paneling on the walls, building a large workbench for the garage, sawing, splitting, and stacking loads of wood for our new woodburner, and we doubled the size of the driveway to accommodate the new garage.

We bought a new Yamaha piano and had it shipped from Muncie. We spent a restful vacation in beautiful southern Indiana and carved a heart with "Pat loves Mary Lee" and two joined women symbols onto the entrance of one of the covered bridges.

Mary Lee's sister Eula Mae ("Tudee") visited us several times and we drove to visit her in Oklahoma, buying the first of our many cowboy hats on the drive back home.

Also during our first decade together, Mary Lee's first two grandchildren, Paul and Sally, were born to Joe and Karen in the early '80s. We never spoke of it, but they both grew up knowing us as a couple.

Mary Lee was granted tenure at IPFW (Indiana-Purdue University at Fort Wayne) the university where she was teaching microbiology to nurses, med-techs, and pre-meds, which meant that she would now have a permanent job here in Fort Wayne. Naturally, we threw a party for her, complete with banners, many guests, refreshments, and a little disco dancing by Joe and me.

Shortly after the party, we had the title of our home legally changed to reflect our joint ownership of it with right of survivorship, so that neither of us would be in danger of losing the home when the other died. Note: all of these legal precautions we took are not needed, for people who are able to have a legal marriage in this country of ours. (We couldn't.)

When my mother, Lois was first getting to know Mary Lee in the late 1970s and had been observing our interaction together over a period of time, she had told Mary Lee in private, "All I know, is that you make my daughter happier than I have ever seen her, and that's enough for me!"

A couple of years later, when Mary Lee was visiting her while she was in the hospital, they had a heart-to-heart conversation, when Mom told Mary Lee, "You're like the sister I always wanted and wished I'd had." Mary Lee was very touched by this and was tearful as she later told me about it.

A few years later, when Lois was terminally ill in the hospital, I had created a twenty-four hour schedule so that each of her family members, including Mary Lee, would come and sit with her, so that if she became confused or frightened, she had someone she knew sitting right there with her. When Lois died in 1982, Mary Lee mourned that loss, as did all of the other members of our family.

A few months after Lois's death, Mary Lee and I pre-planned our own funerals, deciding on cremation for each of us. We purchased both the caskets for the viewing and the burial urns for our ashes. We also decided to share a single plot, and have both of our names engraved on the single headstone. Our burial plot would be just below my mother and father's double plot with their double headstone.

I remember what a momentous and emotional decision it was, when we chose to have a single grave and single headstone. Mary Lee tearfully asked if that's what I really wanted to do, and I firmly said, "Yes! You're my family."

We also hired a lawyer to create our wills, as well as similar Living Wills, and also a Durable Power of Attorney with each of us appointing the other one to be in control of legal and financial matters, in case either one of us was temporarily or permanently incapacitated. Again, necessary precautions for us.

These were some huge steps we took, but we felt very clearly that it was important, and the right thing for us to do. Mom's death had reminded us of the uncertainty of life. I found out many years later, after Mary Lee died, that we also needed to have a Durable Power of Health Directive—which was unknown back in 1983, when we had the other legal work done. But it would have saved me from that legal trauma when she died. I urge you to have this done, if needed in your state!

In 1983, we had another winter with huge amounts of snow, and we inadvertently took a very interesting photo of it, and another of Mary Lee, who was determined to take a ride in the swing.

In 1984, we made a third quilt, this time, together. I actually helped with some of the stitching on this one, since it was for our own bed. Mary Lee referred to it as a little Dutch boy quilt, until I finally declared, "No, it's a little Dutch tomboy quilt!"

Now, thirty years later, in 2014, I still uses it on our bed, and it's beautiful, cheery, and warm.

Young Paul and Sally visited their grandmother in her lab, at IPFW, where she had been engaged in cancer research with mice.

And finally, a little levity to end this chapter—Mary Lee took time out to sand and refinish the top of our aging picnic table in a unique stance and later, when she fell through the broken webbing of the seat of our reclining yard chair . . . of course, I ran into the house to get help—a camera. Notice the obvious expression of appreciation on Mary Lee's face in the picture I took.

Before many days had passed, we had purchased some new webbing material and replaced it on all of our lawn chairs. Since we are both highly educated and somewhat humorless people, we close this chapter with two very serious pictures of each of us, taken in our new family room.

It was a remarkable first decade for us, full of exciting and fun activities, with challenges that we eventually met and overcame, continuing to get to know each other better, as we both changed and grew, and our love and respect continued to deepen. We never sought to change each other; instead, through the years, we continued to learn from each other, often without even realizing it.

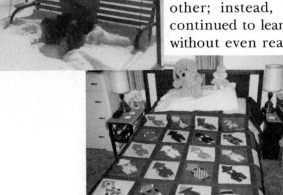

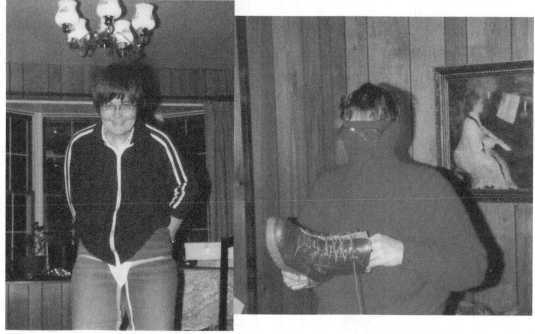

Chapter 5
Our Second Decade: New Traditions Are Begun

January 9, 1985 – December 31, 1994

CHRISTMAS IN CALIFORNIA

December 1984 was our first Christmas celebration in California with all of Danny's family. We began a tradition of me playing for an annual Christmas Eve sing-along with their family and friends at their home; then on Christmas morning, we exchange gifts with Danny and Jannie's family there. Then we all took the freeway to Anaheim, where Danny's parents, Kenny and Pat would host a day-long celebration spending hours of gift-giving/opening and visiting with all of Danny's family.

Danny's parents, Kenny and Pat Davis became good friends to us; they hadn't even met us yet when we flew out for Jan and Danny's wedding, but they invited us to stay in their home while we were there. Kenny had served in World War II, and Pat was his war bride, from England. We enjoyed a warm friendship with them for many years.

Another tradition started by Mary Lee and me: on the day before we would fly back home from California, the two of us would

walk just one block away from Jannie's home into an unattended orange grove, and proceed to fill our winter coat pockets with a bunch of oranges to take home with us. We never picked them off of the trees—we just took the good ones that had fallen on the ground.

Hmmm, first, we had filched corn in Muncie, now we're filching oranges in California . . . seems like we have just a tad bit of sneaky larceny hidden somewhere, not very deep in our psyches; loved the excitement of it, maybe?

> *Once, we told each other goodbye, not knowing if we were going to soon die together*

A PIVOTAL EXPERIENCE FOR US

On one of those annual flights to California, as we began to prepare for landing, our pilot announced that there was a potentially serious problem: The display for the front wheel on our plane was not working, and they couldn't tell what the position of the wheel was.

If it was pointed straight forward, there would be no problem. However, if it was turned even a slight angle either way, there was a strong possibility that the plane might flip upside down as soon as that wheel touched the ground. It was a large plane (727) filled with about a hundred passengers aboard.

They told us we needed to prepare for the worst and asked us to remove our glasses, bend forward in our seats, and assume the crash position with our heads down and our arms protecting ourselves. Faced with this possibly dangerous situation, everyone was very quiet.

The pilot also announced that we would not be landing at our assigned gate, but rather farther out on the tarmac, where they already had fire engines and ambulances and medical personnel positioned, ready and waiting for us, in case they were needed.

Mary Lee and I turned to each other as we crouched there, saying softly to each other that if this was the way it was going to end for us, that it was okay. We'd had a good run, and if this was going to mean our death, we were okay with going together. We quietly said our goodbyes to each other in case this was indeed going to be the end of our time together; we kissed and professed our mutual love, and holding hands, waited quietly and calmly for whatever would occur. We trusted and believed that whatever did happen would be for our highest good.

We landed safely, but were profoundly changed by the experience.

Other highlights of our lives during this decade:

From 1983 to 1986, I finally realized the dream I'd had ever since I had been in eighth grade—to teach music and choirs in high school. For the first time, I was directing a swing choir and teaching them choreography, now working with older students and more developed and accomplished singers. I started with a group of nine girls, added nine boys, a pianist and other accompanists, and the choir began winning trophies and awards in the many contests they entered. One senior was so excited as he carried a large trophy above his head, exclaiming, "This is the first trophy we've won in four years!"

If any readers have ever seen the recent TV show called *Glee*, believe it or not, in 1983, I had already renamed our Woodlan High School swing choir New Directions, over twenty years before the TV show choir had that same name! I laughed when I first heard their name. However, that high school job entailed lots of evening rehearsals and many weekend performances, and I found myself yearning to be home with Mary Lee more—so I returned to teach at New Haven Jr. High School for my final nine years of teaching young people.

In 1986, Mary Lee travelled alone to her hometown in Henryetta, Oklahoma and spent a memorable time with her brother Theon and her sister Eula (she had called her "Tudee" as a child, and still did.) Theon joked with them, saying, "I'm the boss, 'cause I'm the oldest." He was only eleven months older than Mary Lee. They all enjoyed their time together; it turned out to be the last visit Mary Lee had with her brother before his sudden and unexpected death during a very hard winter. She underwent the trauma of not even being able to travel to his funeral, because the airport was closed down due to an ice storm that covered our area. She always cherished her memories of their special time together.

For several years we had been attending the National Women's Music Festival on the Indiana University campus in Bloomington. Three separate times, we had bought matching rings, hand made by Jane Iris, a creator of fine jewelry who travelled to the festival from California.

We had become devoted fans of Katherine V. Forrest and had bought, read, and re-read every book in the large collection that she had authored over the years. Her first book, *Curious Wine*, became an extremely popular classic lesbian novel and has had many printings over the years. We had even written to her, expressing our great admiration for her writing.

In 1986, she was a guest speaker for a writer's workshop at the festival. When she entered the tiered amphitheater, the audience gave her a prolonged standing ovation, which I believe startled and amazed her. She may not have realized how many of us in that packed hall enthusiastically supported her writings.

Mary Lee, Katherine V. Forrest, Pat

We had an opportunity to visit with her and discovered that we shared the same anniversary date of January 9! Over the years, we exchanged many cards and letters. Once, when Mary Lee wrote in a letter to her that I was lascivious, our next letter from Katherine began, "Dear Mary Lee and lascivious Pat," and we both burst out laughing. Over the years, Katherine has always been incredibly kind, generous, loving, and extremely supportive of us and of our love, and her letters and notes never failed to make our hearts swell with joy.

Beginning in 1987, we visited my growing family in Elko, Nevada every four years or so, meeting new babies every time; Teri had a total of nine children and home-schooled them all.

One year we saw the Basque festival and parade, learning to drink wine their way.

We even watched a contest of Basque "yelling," which sounded remarkably like the war cry of Lucy Lawless, on the *Xena, Warrior Princess* TV show!

Twenty-seven years later, when we had a Deihl family reunion in Elko in 2014, there were already twenty-two Deihl family members living in that area by then!

In 1988, with the help of Danny (Jannie's husband,) we travelled to Los Angeles, shopped for, and purchased our gold wedding bands for our thirteenth anniversary. Thank you, Danny!

May, 1991—Katie Davis was born to Jan and Danny. Mary Lee flew to California to help Jannie.

As a toddler, Katie couldn't pronounce "grandma," so she called Mary Lee "Mawcaw." Even as young women, she and her younger sister Julie continued to refer to her as their Mawcaw. Mary Lee was always amused by that affectionate name.

At IPFW (where Mary Lee was a professor) we took a Women's Studies course called "Women and Religion"; it was very eye-opening and illuminating, informing our faith.

Early in this decade, Mary Lee took a sabbatical leave from IPFW to work in Muncie at Ball State University on further research with her primary professor, Dr. Alice Bennett. The semester of separation would be difficult for both of us, but especially for her, since she wouldn't be at home.

Mary Lee moaned, "How will I ever be able to fall asleep at night, without your right shoulder to pillow my head?" Kinda like Xena and Gabrielle slept by the campfire, only on the other shoulder. We bought a large, incredibly soft yellow panda bear, and named it Rosie, after Katherine Hepburn's character in the *The African Queen*, a movie we loved to watch together. I suggested that she might be able to lay her head on Rosie's soft body every night and think of me; and that she could hug her, too. Really . . . we did that.

For my part, I took a roll of toilet paper, counted exactly how many days she would be gone, and numbered (with a black felt-tipped pen) that many squares on the roll, then rolled it back onto the empty cardboard tube in reverse order, with the largest number on top. Next to the bottom number, I had printed "Welcome home, Babboo!" Yup, we had become each other's "sweet babboo," just like in the Peanuts cartoons. When I finished it, I put it into her suitcase, with a note saying that the last thing she should do every night would be to tear off the square on the outside of the roll and flush it down the toilet, saying, "There's another day down the drain!"

That way, she could always see how many days of separation were still left and would be encouraged to see the numbers getting smaller each night. She laughed and said she would certainly perform that little ritual each night, and that it would help her. A couple of big babies, huh?

My brother Bud had been a professor and Dean of Fine Arts at several universities, and we attended his inauguration as President Charles ("Bud") Deihl of the Kendall College of Art and Design.

After Theon Radebaugh's death, Mary Lee's extended family began having Radebaugh Cousins' Reunions in Oklahoma every three years. One year, they even had t-shirts made!

Then five of Mary Lee's family formed a singing group, which sang at one of the Radebaugh reunions in Oklahoma and also at our Unity church in Fort Wayne, Indiana. I invented the unusual name of the group, with the first two letters of each person's first name, in the order of when they came into the family: eg., Mary Lee, Jan, Joe, Pat, and Danny—or, The MaJaJoPaDa Singers!

By the way, we were really good, and we learned and recorded several songs.

MORE ENJOYABLE TRADITIONS
TRIPS TO SHIPSHEWANA

Back in Indiana, almost every summer, we would drive seventy or eighty miles to Shipshewana, Indiana, into Amish country in the northern part of Indiana. We loved going up there and managed to go almost every year, sometimes with friends. We usually came home with wonderful-tasting fruits and vegetables, home-made jellies and jams, and *way* too much of their delicious baked goods, from bread to cookies and pies, and other tasty delights.

While there, we bought everything from clothes to antiques, to any kind of unique treasures. I would often buy little t-shirts for many of my great nieces and great nephews, with a picture or message on each one that was especially meaningful for each of them. I always had to do some research on their sizes and current interests every year. We usually had lunch there at one of three small buildings with food and picnic tables; my favorite was their sloppy joes, and sometimes we'd get ice cream or a piece of pie.

Once, we bought wooden birds, flowers, and hearts that we would eventually fasten onto the door of the new shed we had built, with Joe's help.

Another time, during our first years together, we bought two black, wrought-iron wall decorations which, more than twenty years later, still hang over the doorway from our kitchen into the family room which proclaim:

"To love and be loved is the greatest joy on earth."
and
"Grow old along with me; the best is yet to be."

. . . and it certainly was.

NASHVILLE, INDIANA

The summer of 1982, we took the first of many vacations in Nashville, Indiana, where we would enjoy sightseeing in the many shops. We discovered one named Yesteryear Tintype Photos, where we would put on costumes and pose for an old-fashioned picture. Our first one endeavor was of two strong-willed and armed cowgirls, that we dubbed Belle Starr and Calamity Jane. We later fastened a brass label to the wooden frame that warned "Don't mess with us feminists!" We even gave a smaller

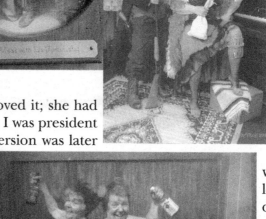

version of it to my mom, and she loved it; she had even become a NOW member when I was president of the local chapter. That smaller version was later given to my younger sister, Jan Blain.

Some of the other tintypes we had taken over the years were of Civil War times, a couple of drunken old women in a tub of water with guns and whiskey, and a wedding picture. We laughed a lot each time, and sometimes we found it difficult to keep a solemn, serious face while they were taking the picture.

Several years, we also bought beautiful matching rings from a jeweler's shop there.

Then one year, the weather was dangerously hot while we were there—the outdoor temperature was over a hundred degrees, with high humidity. We were careful to spend most of our time in places that were air conditioned, but when we arrived at the Yesteryear shop, they apologized to us, saying that their air conditioning was broken.

We said that we certainly wouldn't be donning any heavy costumes this time, and we were disappointed. Then, they showed us an album full of possible pictures that could be used, and we pointed at one of them, saying, "That's the one we'll do—that will work!"

In the two pictures we look like we're sitting in a tub of water, naked, but actually, we each were wearing shorts and a tube top under the boas that they draped around us. Mine looks like it slipped down a little.

Then they handed us each a couple of props: a whiskey bottle and a weapon. As they prepared to take our picture, we said to each other, "Let's look like a couple of mean and dangerous drunks." And we did. Then, we asked them to take one more, where we'd look like happy, drunken fools. And we did.

I don't know what year we had our last photo taken there, but I remember looking through that photo book again, and when we came to one of the possible pictures, I said to Mary Lee, "Hey, since Indiana law doesn't allow us to become legally married, let's have a wedding picture taken this time!" Mary Lee took one look at it and said, "I'm *not* putting on that wedding gown!" To which I immediately replied, "That's okay, I'll wear the gown, and you can be the groom."

And here's a picture you probably never thought you'd see!

Especially if you knew us.

OUR CHURCH—and CHOIR

In 1985, we joined the Unity Church in Fort Wayne. We had felt incredibly welcomed by the people, and on our first Sunday visiting there in 1984, we had been astounded to hear the minister use the phrase "Mother/Father God." After the service, we sat tearfully in our car, holding hands and declared to each other, "We're home!" We've continued to be active members there.

With the help of Bonnie Stephan and Jean Roth, who each were our church pianist/organist/soloist, I formed the first choir that Unity had ever had.

It grew from seven members to almost forty during the eight years that I was the music director/choir director. At the beginning we sang just two or three parts, but eventually we were singing eight-part a cappella works! Our first robes were wine-colored and homemade, and we later purchased ivory robes and stoles;

Jean, Bonnie, Pat

we needed to use both kinds of robes for our large choir.

For several years, we held an overnight "choir intensive" in the early fall, a retreat to kick off the new season. It was an effective and fun way for us to welcome new members, become more bonded through planned activities, and have an opportunity to read through the songs we would be singing during that year. The members were incredibly trusting of my teaching and directing, faithful in attendance, and filled with love and positive energy. I felt so honored to lead them—and my Mary Lee was a charter member of the group. What fun!

Our choir motto, as in all of my choirs, was:

"None of us can do alone what we can do together"

Later, I learned about something I had never heard of or imagined.

SOUL RETRIEVAL

Years ago, in a conversation with a good friend and minister, I shared with Rev. Carolyn Christie that it had always seemed strange and troubling to me that I had almost no memories of my childhood. With her extensive knowledge of things of the spirit, she suggested I might want to get in touch with Laurie Rainey Schmidt, an experienced counselor and also a shamanic practitioner in Fort Wayne.

When I met her, she gave me an informational brochure about "signs of soul loss" and led me to a book titled *Soul Retrieval*, so I could educate myself about it and determine if I needed her help. It seems that *if* a part of your soul has left your body because of a physical or emotional trauma, it can block your memories of that part of your past with it. It seemed very strange and odd to me, but I had the attitude of "Who knows? It just might help, so I'll give it a try." I had never heard of this before.

SHAMANISM

Shamanism is an ancient cross-cultural discipline for learning and healing which recognizes and honors the interdependence of all living things. A shaman is a person of compassion and high ethical standards who is adept at traveling the sacred territories of non-ordinary reality and who works on behalf of all those who ask for help. In other words, they can enter the spirit world and communicate with the souls there, both animal and human.

When I arrived for my appointment, Laurie told me there would be a spirit guide that would help her in her search, and after her journey, she said that for me it was a mother wolf with pups. That healing was so touching and evident to me, that I have since had a special place in my heart for wolves.

Once, in Shipshewana, I even found a unique license plate with a wolf's head on it. I used to have it on the front of my car. I even had them add the words spirit guide to it.

After the horrible crash in 2010, I gave the wolf plate away and instead, I reclaimed from Mary Lee's ruined car the other plate I had purchased in Shipshewana as a gift for Mary Lee. It now is on the front of my car, and it is a more apt description of my life today. (see page 125)

In 1991 we had our second large addition built onto our home. We tripled the size of our small bedroom, including in it a library with five large bookcases, an entertainment center, with several smaller cases around it, two new nightstands, a new headboard and frame for our bed, and another shower/bath. And we built everything ourselves . . . except for the bath.

We were becoming experts at assembling Sauder furniture. We also had another large bay window added to our bedroom, to match the one we'd had built in 1980, in the new family room at the other end of the house. And in another of our traditions, once more, we'd saved lots of money over time, and we were able to pay our builders in three payments, just like we'd done for the 1980 addition—no loan, and no interest to pay. We were grateful we could do that.

In May, 1993, Mary Lee retired from IPFW, where she had been a Professor of Microbiology for sixteen years. She was now Professor Emerita, but they asked her to continue teaching through the summer and the fall, since her replacement was not able to fill her position yet. Mary Lee was respected and loved by her many students over the years. She taught a very difficult course to pre-meds, med techs, biology majors,

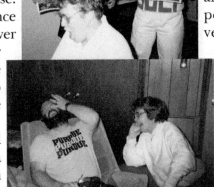

and nurses, and did all she could to help them learn the vital material and pass her courses and labs. She inspired many to go on in the medical field, and she also inspired older students, especially when they learned that she had received her doctorate degree when she was fifty-three years old—she always encouraged them, saying, "It's never too late!"

Mary Lee's son Joe and granddaughter Sally were there for all of the festivities, and I believe that Margie and Larry, my sister and brother-in-law were also there. I have always regretted that I didn't take the whole day off from my teaching duties, so that I could have been there for the whole celebration. Mary Lee didn't say anything, but I always felt I had disappointed her by arriving late on that very important day.

During a visit by Jannie to Indiana, the three of us had lots of fun hamming up our state song, "Back Home Again in Indiana" with the help of placemats showing Indiana scenes of sycamore trees, fields of hay, and the Wabash River.

And it's really unfortunate that Joe and his mom never had a sense of humor, and never, ever shared a laugh.

During the latter part of this decade, we visited the Chicago Museum of History with Joe and Sally, and we enjoyed clowning around with the dinosaurs and giant furniture there.

In the mid—'70s and '80s, whenever we could, we disco danced to almost anything by the Bee Gees ("Stayin' Alive," "More Than a Woman To Me,") and Donna Summers,

It was good exercise, fun, and a very social activity for us.

Jo Stafford had recorded a song called "No Other Love," with a melody by Fredric Chopin. When Mary Lee was feeling really good about things, she would often spontaneously begin singing at home, often without realizing it. I usually didn't say anything at the time because I didn't want her to feel obvious or stop singing, which always made me happy, too. I often told her I loved to hear her sing, and that her voice sounded very much like Jo Stafford's. It really did!

Whenever we heard Neil Diamond singing "Sweet Caroline" on the radio, I'd sing along, but each time, I would substitute "Sweet Mary Lee," instead. She always got a kick out of that.

I forgot . . . in 1980, we bought a swing for the back yard, and many evenings when the weather was nice, we would gently rock in the swing as we harmonized on many of the old, old songs that we both knew from our childhoods, even though sometimes her Oklahoma version might differ just a little from my Indiana version . . . We always enjoyed making music together. Even at church, we always harmonized on the hymns. Often, people sitting in front of us were amused and sometimes made positive comments about our singing.

Very early in our time together, we developed the habit of her sitting on my right side, so that even after an operation on my left shoulder, I could still put my right arm around her. Also, whenever we shared a meal with family or friends, we sat at the table the same way, because she was right-handed and I was left-handed—and that way, we could unobtrusively hold hands under the table while we ate. We loved holding hands but wanted to do it more subtly.

We were very much in the closet to almost everyone in our lives, with just a very few exceptions.

> **"Wish We Didn't Have to Meet . . . Secretly"**

After we both retired from teaching at the close of our second decade together, we began very gradually to be more relaxed in certain situations where we felt safe, such as at our church, where we sometimes held hands—but on the seat of the pew, where it wasn't noticed—or one of us would have our arm around the other's shoulders—but on the back of the pew. Even after her death, friends noticed that I always left a space on my right side for her, and I still put my arm on the back of the pew where she would have sat. It touched me that they noticed and affectionately remarked on it.

The summer of 1993, I had to have a shoulder operation, and I stopped directing the Unity Church Choir at that time. However, when I had almost recovered, we had a large choir party, and besides being a wonderful celebration, it also became the birth of a new choir—a community choir—The Celebration Singers! And they've now been singing together for more than two decades!

During this second decade together, we became even closer and trusting friends; our respect and love became deeper and more enduring—no more uncertainties about how long we'd be together—we knew it would be for the rest of our lives!

We continued to admire and appreciate each other and to learn from each other. This is probably the decade when we began to repeatedly declare to each other, "You're God's greatest gift to me!" and also "You're such a miracle to me!"

And we also continued to have a rich and varied life, enjoying our sweet and impish inner child, our thoughtful and responsible inner adult, and the daily wonder of living our lives with a good, gentle, authentic and loving life partner.

Matching t-shirts at a Radebaugh Reunion in Henryetta, Olahoma.

Chapter 6
Our Third Decade

1995 – Dec. 31, 2004

"I Just Fall in Love Again"

Once, in a booth somewhere, they made this computer-generated "photo" of us, by using lighter and darker rectangles, like the really ancient printers used to use, probably on an Apple Computer. Not sure when it was done, but as you can see, we were certainly much younger then; I just found this computer picture in our piano bench, where it was kept safe among all that music, for who knows how many years!

THE FIRST OF THREE LARGE PARTIES

January 15, 1995, was Mary Lee's seventieth birthday, and she was ill, probably just getting over a lung infection and not feeling well at all. We were sitting in our bedroom, reading in our side-by-side chairs and sometimes resting on the bed. Because I was on the lookout, I spied my sister Margie standing out in the hallway. I quietly went over and nodded at her, then closed the door.

That morning, I had gone out and put up a large banner in our front yard, letting people know what was going on, and I took a picture of it—the first of many that would be taken that day.

Mary Lee never saw that sign, because she didn't feel like leaving our bedroom.

A few weeks prior, I had secretly mailed many invitations to friends and family members, asking them to RSVP to my sister Margie, stressing that it was to be a surprise party for Mary Lee, but not for me. Right after putting up the sign in the front yard, I also taped on top of the doorbell instructions on the front door and also in the living room, so that the arriving guests would just come in and not talk or make any noise as they deposited their coats in another room and moved quietly into the family room and took a seat.

Several people (including Margie) had come an hour early to put up lots of decorations, set up a large birthday cake for her with seventy candles on it, and a smaller (chocolate) cake for our anniversary, with another twenty candles on it, and lots of other refreshments on the large table.

They also set up many folding chairs, and several other people were designated to light all ninety candles when given the signal and turn off all the lights in the family room. Each guest took a chair and sat quietly while they waited for our entrance.

When everything was ready and all the guests had arrived, Margie sneaked back to our bedroom door

and gave me the signal. I had earlier suggested to my Murdy (while all this had been going on) that she might feel a little better if she put on one of her nice-looking outfits, and if she felt like it, we might go for a short walk, since we'd been cooped up in the bedroom for several hours. Trusting soul that she was, she complied, possibly not even realizing that it was her birthday.

PAT DIRECTS TWO NEW, ADULT CHOIRS

In 1993, while still teaching, Pat organized a community choir which later was called the Celebration Singers. They began singing at churches, then retirement homes and nursing homes and assorted banquets, even sang the "Star-Spangled Banner" at a hockey game in the Fort Wayne coliseum, and sang Christmas carols in the Fort Wayne Police Headquarters one year. We had a police officer in the choir at the time. They were fun and became quite versatile, singing programs with a large variety of songs, including sing-alongs, mystery songs (with a prize awarded for the correct title), kids songs (with silly kids' hats,) cowboy songs (with hats), patriotic songs, old-fashioned songs (with 1920 skimmers), interesting arrangements of religious songs, Disney songs, Richard Rodgers songs from musicals, etc.

Many of them, when joining the choir, said, "I don't sing very well, but I love to sing." And without fail I would respond, "You're the kind of person I want in my choir, one who loves to sing." I always figured that I could teach them to sing better, in time. Over the years, we built a reputation for being a really good choir that gave entertaining programs; our audiences grew, and a funded organization called Audiences Unlimited began to schedule concerts for us and paid us for each concert. Now we had an income, to purchase (and make) unique choir outfits, props (like hats), and folders and new music each year.

2015 will be their twenty-second year of performing and touching peoples' lives in a very positive way. Once, after a concert, we were told by two women that the friend they were sitting with hadn't spoken for several years . . . but she sang with us during the sing-along song! We had chills and were amazed at the almost miraculous effect our music could have on people. The choir is very much in demand for their entertaining and versatile programs, now.

In June, 1995, I retired from thirty-four years of teaching music and choirs in various grade levels in different schools in the East Allen County School System. At my last spring Concert at New Haven Middle School, the Celebration Singers also took part as a guest choir, joining the kids to sing several songs, including "The Lion Sleeps Tonight" and "The Blessing of Aaron," a benediction we always sang at the end of our concerts.

During that concert, I announced to the audience and to the one-hundred-and-fifty choir members standing behind me on the risers, that I had taught my students many lessons over the years, but that I had also learned from them.

I said, "I believe that life is all about learning, and now, it's time for me to learn some new lessons. I don't know yet what I'd be doing, but I hope it will have to do with music, and I know it's gonna be great!"

Then, just one month after my retirement, a prestigious Fort Wayne choir had a search committee to find a new director. Helen Donnell had formed The Festival Choir of Peace and Understanding ten years earlier, and was now retiring as director. I was chosen to be their new director, and they're now in their twentieth season with me as director.

The first year I directed them, we had been taking pictures of the choir in their formal gowns, and I suggested we might also have a gag photo taken, too. Many of them entered into the spirit of the fun or laughed at the silliness of the rest of us.

At the request of one of the choir members, I began a Prison Ministry with the choir that first year, giving concerts at women's prisons and men's prisons in Michigan and Indiana each spring. We also have been donating whatever the chaplain tells us they need that year. The Festival choir continues that ministry today. We are known as "The musical arm of the Associated Churches of Allen County, Indiana." It continues to be made up of choir directors and choir members from about twenty different churches in the area. Jay Heare has joined us, and we are now co-directors of this choir.

The members of both of these choirs are wonderful people: talented and dedicated, kind and generous, thoughtful and loving, hard-working and faithful. They make my life incredibly rich and fulfilling, and directing them has become a main passion in my life.

FAMILY REUNIONS

After Mary Lee's brother Theon's death, her family decided it was important for their whole extended family (a very large group) to get together and keep in touch on a regular basis. So in 1988, they held their first of many Radebaugh Cousins' Reunions every three years, with the first several in Henryetta, Oklahoma, where all the older cousins had grown up.

Professional photos were taken of each family group, with one large picture of everyone there. Most of the older cousin's families were fairly large.Each reunion, the gathering grew larger and larger.

In March, 1997 my dad, Elmer, died, and many of the Deihl family members came to attend his funeral. Six cousins (out of eight) who attended got to know one another, almost twenty years after all those kids in the Christmas photos had been taken

every year, and they discovered they enjoyed getting reacquainted as adults. Many of them returned to Fort Wayne three months later to celebrate the wedding of Margie and Larry's daughter Roxanne to Jeff Tuesley.

In October, 1999 Jonathon (Margie and Larry's son) whose family now lived in Texas, organized the first Deihl Reunion, which was held in Elko, NV. Family members from four of the Deihl siblings attended; we missed Jan and John Blain and the group from the eastern states, but some members had never met before, and it was a great beginning. It took fifteen years before our next one.

MORE OF MARY LEE'S FAMILY

In February, 1995, Mary Lee's last grandchild, Julia Davis, was born. Over the years, Julie and her whole family (Danny, Jannie, Katie and Julie) became proficient and were active in the performing arts (dancing, singing, acting) and have developed a professional stage presence and strong capabilities in that area. Both Katie and Julie have become intelligent, beautiful young women, inside and out. Mary Lee and I are both very proud of them.

Paul Richeson and his sister Sally (Cates) are now each married and living out of state with their spouses. Also, Paul and Sara now have Owen, who is Mary Lee's first great-grandson.

Deihl family reunion, Elko, Nevada 1999

HAWAIIAN CRUISE

December, 1997—Neither of us had ever been on a cruise before, and we decided to go with bunches of other lesbians and lesbian-friendly people on an Olivia Cruise around some of the Hawaiian Islands.

As it turned out, we would be aboard a ship with six hundred other lesbians! A first for us, and the crew and staff often told us how much they loved and appreciated us, saying that we were more upbeat, ready for fun, and more cooperative and flexible than the sometimes power hungry and demanding regular passengers.

We paid for this cruise gradually, over fourteen months, interest free. Again, our way of financing the big expenses.

We took helicopter rides over a rain forest, then later over an active volcano; we walked in a rain forest with huge plants and flowers, were greeted at one island with a huge banner and the mayor welcoming us, and received leis and kisses on the cheek on another island. We attended a Hawaiian church service on Sunday, and had a hula lesson during a boat trip. I had my first experience snorkeling.

Mary Lee took a watercolor painting workshop, which inspired her to begin painting again for the first time in many years. The next fall, she began to paint Christmas cards every year for our families and friends.

And every Olivia Cruise has a commitment ceremony.

So many new and wonderful experiences—and we could even hold hands on board! People just smiled at us, and many of them were holding hands, too.

We knew that at some point in the near future, we wanted to have a commitment ceremony in our own church, with a religious ceremony. That seed had now been planted.

In May, 1998, I was diagnosed with uterine cancer and had a successful operation to remove it all. We caught it early, and there were no chemo or radiation treatments needed.

Then in August, 1998, Mary Lee awoke me in the middle of the night; she was experiencing a heart attack. At the hospital, they ran numerous tests and eventually found that it was the result of a blood clot from her irregular heartbeats, so she needed no further operations.

However, she went through rehabilitation and the classes to help people *not* have another heart attack.

Being pro-active, we bought a treadmill that each of us used to exercise regularly. Soon after, Mary Lee and I began to share our very own personal trainer, Brittany Coughlin, at the YWCA. I had already been working out with personal trainers for a few years.

Later, we had different trainers. We began scheduling our workouts at the same time, with two excellent personal trainers who also happened to be good friends with each other.

Sue Bair and Kate Black also became wonderful and loving friends to us over the ensuing years, always helping us both to be more healthy, flexible, and stronger than we would have otherwise been, especially at our increasing ages.

The following year at a memorial service for Claudette Farone, our former pastor, who had died from a brain tumor, one speaker quoted something Claudette had urged:

"If there's something you really want to do, just go ahead and do it, because you really don't know how much time you're going to have in this life."

Mary Lee and I looked at each other and quietly agreed that now was the time for us to think seriously about finally having the "joining" ceremony we'd thought about over the years.

"Why Ya' Gotta Be So Rude? I'm Gonna Marry Her, Anyway!"
"Goin' To the Chapel, and We're . . . Gonna Get Married"
"I Want To Thank You for Being My Wife"

OUR WEDDING

We began by affirming that everything would be in Divine Order—all the decisions we would be making, from who to invite, who to have help us plan and print the invitations, who we would ask to conduct our ceremony, working together to compose the service, who would be the photographer, who would supply the flowers and food, who would help during the reception afterwards, who would take part in the service itself, and all the other details to work out and finalize. We found that we were already in agreement about each task, and it was all completed in peace, joy, and in an orderly fashion . . . with God's help, we planned and prepared for a large, formal wedding in just three months!

We had over a hundred guests who attended, bringing with them only positive, joy-filled energy, with many flying in (or driving) from different states, as far west as California and Oklahoma and Texas, and as far east as Ohio, Pennsylvania, and New York—and of course, several others driving in from different cities in Indiana.

Looking through piles of miscellaneous photographs for this book, I was astonished to find a hand-written copy of my Mary Lee's wedding vows, and I wept as I read them:

Pat, my dear friend, my dear partner, my mate,
For 25 years I have loved you, I have loved you closely, secretly,
against reason, and always, always against traditional wisdom.
We have already been up many hills and down many valleys together.
For 25 years we have tested our vows to each other,
our quiet, secret vows, and we know we are one.
I promise to hold you close the rest of my life, and I am honored to affirm
my promises to you
before God and before our families and friends, I will love you always.

"Some People Wait a Lifetime for a Moment Like This"

Could I Have This Dance for the Rest of My Life?

MANY, MANY MATCHING T-SHIRTS, ETC.

Mary Lee and I found it was often fun to wear matching outfits, especially t-shirts and sweatshirts. We freely (and not too subtly) showed to anyone and everyone, by our appearance, that "we b'langs together." We very often bought matching sets of rings, necklaces, pins, and other wearing apparel, and we usually discussed what we'd wear to different functions and events.

We were very proud of the other, and often said so to each other. I think we both liked the sense of belonging together when in public, and I believe that we were both more socially secure and more at ease in all situations, to not have to say in words what we said by our appearance.

You've already seen the matching Hillary shirts and the many matching t-shirts we purchased over the years, many at the Xena Conventions. Later, several of the matching holiday sweatshirts were purchased each year at Walgreens Drugstores!

I recently had a flashback of a childhood memory that may shed some light about my earliest experiences of wearing matching t-shirts. When I was young, my brother Bud and I were about the same size, even though he was two years older than I. For some reason, Mom had bought a couple of sets of matching, striped t-shirts; I think that was something she hadn't done before. Or after.

I really liked my older brother; I looked up to him, and on some childish level, maybe I wanted to be like him. My oldest brother, Bob shared a bedroom with Bud when we were all young, and my bedroom door was right next to theirs. Sometimes in the morning, I would lean over and peek into their room to see what kind of t-shirt Bud was going to wear that day. Then, I'd get out the same kind and put it on. When we went out in public, strangers would ask if we were twins. I felt proud of their assumption, but I think Bud was not happy with his little sister. He reminded me recently that he would then go back into his room and change his shirt, but that I would go back and change mine, too. I don't know how often this happened, but we both have memories of it happening more than once.

Courtesy of The Fort Wayne, IN News-Sentinel

Today, I found a newspaper clipping in one of the old photo albums, which showed four kids, ages seven or eight to ten. The caption under the photo stated, "It's an old custom, bobbing for apples on Halloween night. It's a 'damp' feeling of satisfaction to corner the elusive apple in a tub of water, as Bud Deihl shows. Others having fun are, left to right, Judy Clark, Patty Deihl (Bud's sister,) and Jeffery Clark, Judy's brother."

Guess what Bud and I are wearing for the picture? The photo was in the newspaper on October 27, 1948, just two days before my ninth birthday.

To my memory, as an adult, I never again had a desire—a need—to dress the same as another adult . . . until Mary Lee.

"Ain't It Fun, Ain't It Fun"

"There's a Place for Us... Somewhere"

XENA, WARRIOR PRINCESS CONVENTIONS

The *Xena* TV series began in 1995, and we discovered it a year or two later. I was somewhat put off by the modern language used in a show set in ancient times. I also felt the same way about the *Hercules* shows, which had begun airing earlier. I wouldn't have watched either show, but Mary Lee was intrigue by the *Xena* show and wanted to watch it. So we began following a comic book type of show with some over-acting and scripts that weren't all that great.

As time went on, the scripts and storylines became better, in my mind. We both agreed that the acting improved by leaps and bounds, being more subtle and believable. Sometimes the story and dialogue were funny, sometimes frightening or tragic, and later the writers and actors began having a lot of fun with subtext, especially about Xena and Gabrielle's relationship. Some fans of the show thought there was no subtext, and others caught every look, every word, and every gesture—and thoroughly enjoyed each reference. We were, of course, in the latter group.

Then, the scripts began dealing with different religions, good forces vs. bad, and frequently dealt with historical characters, such as Caesar, Brutus, and characters from the Old Testament of the Bible, and from the very beginning of the show, they protrayed many of the Greek gods: Ares, Athena, Aphrodite, Zeus, etc. By this time, we were hooked on the show and watched it regularly.

By December, 1999, I had already noticed an ad for Xena merchandise printed at the end of a show, and I sent for something and received a catalog and a free t-shirt. By Christmas, I gave Mary Lee several gifts that were all about Xena.

We both kept purchasing through the years, and finally, we owned almost everything in the catalogues—VHS tapes of each season (and later, DVDs,), t-shirts, mugs, hats, letter openers, luggage, jewelry, leather jackets, satin jackets, and sweatshirts. I had one that said "Xena" on it, and hers said "Gabrielle." Pacifists that we were, we even bought a Xena sword that still hangs above the mantle in our family room. Later, we also purchased a set of Gabrielle's sais.

Then, Mary Lee noticed the small print at the end of one show; we copied down the contact information and made arrangements to attend our first Xena Convention in May, 2001. By that time they were no longer filming the TV show, but we understand that 2001 was one of the largest gatherings they'd had. Two years later, we learned about the gold seats, and we began buying the more expensive tickets so that our seats were now much closer to the front of the large convention hall.

The stars and other cast members, writers, and directors would come onstage and answer questions of the fans; some of the cast would perform at a talent show; autograph photos from the show; or have their pictures taken with the fans. We did all of that. Mary Lee would sometimes relax at home by watching many of the shows from our collection of all six seasons of the show, many times repeating some of her favorites.

We would often watch them together—stories about the beliefs and practices of the religions of different countries of the world, stories of faith, bravery and turmoil, of evil forces and angels, of eternal love and soulmates—even stories of reincarnation, heaven and hell.

Mary Lee, who was a professor of microbiology at a university, was often the analytical, skeptical scientist about spiritual things and would sometimes say, "I wish I had your faith, Pat." But because we both loved the two main characters and often watched those stories with spiritual leanings, we both began to be more open to some of the concepts of their faith, the nature of life and love, and even the eternal life of souls.

We were sometimes deeply touched by the stories, and we didn't realize it, but we were learning more about their faith and, in turn, developing a deeper faith ourselves. It taught us about courage and mutual support during adversity, and that love really can be eternal.

In the end, the *Xena* shows had a powerful, profoundly positive influence on our faith. Attending

Renée O'Connor and Lucy Lawless

With Renée O'Connor

these eleven conventions was one of the best things we did for ourselves. It was a place where we felt safe to hold hands, have fun, and become friends with other fans over the years, including a couple of special couples. We got to visit with the stars and over the years, they gradually came to know us. Many of the fans we met were pleasantly surprised at how long we'd been together and that we still had such a loving and respectful and playful relationship after so many years. We seemed to become mini-celebrities to some, and a very positive role model to many Xena fans.

Sonja Pospisil, a friend from Austria, sent me this e-mail in 2014: "I feel blessed that I had known you and Mary Lee as one of the most beautiful and impressive couples I have ever met . . . I had always loved seeing you together! You brought so much joy and love to our Xena family, and now you continue, inspired by Mary Lee, by writing your story! What a gift for all of us."

With Anita Ellis

With Terrina Jones and Linda Bywater

With Erika Balderson and Rhys Miller

Mary Lee and Hudson Leick

With Michael Hurst

With David Franklin

With Jennifer Ward-Lealand

Late in 2003, I was diagnosed with a slow-growing tumor (meningioma) on my brain, near my left optic nerve. In February, 2004, a team was set to do a stereotactic surgery (highly focused radiation) to kill the tumor, before it grew large enough to create symptoms in me.

We discovered that one of our Festival Choir members, Dr. John Agnew, would be the physicist on the team, largely responsible for creating on the computer the plan to determine how long, where, and when to administer the radiation. We always knew John was kind and unassuming, and now we also knew that he was brilliant and highly skilled.

"You Are the Wind Beneath My Wings"

In order to create this plan, the doctors had to literally screw a steel helmet into my skull, even with the pain shots they gave me, it was a very painful procedure. Then they fastened the helmet to the x-ray machine so I couldn't move my head while they gave me a CT scan. I held my little stuffed wolf, Ares, under my folded hands, to keep my arms from flopping off of the table.

Dana and Rev. Carolyn Christie, and Wendy McNeil Shackley pray with us

Figuring out the plan took many hours to do; I wore that helmet for nine hours; the actual radiation took only about fifteen minutes. Mary Lee was with me the whole day, empathizing with me, because she knew I was in a great deal of pain. I've had many MRI's over the past ten years, and that tumor is definitely dead.

Ironically, about a week before this operation, I also had a severe and dangerous allergic reaction to a statin drug (taken to bring cholesterol down.) Eventually, it got so bad that I couldn't walk normally, I couldn't dress herself, and I could barely feed myself—and we didn't know if this would be permanent.

I had profound numbness from my toes to my knees, and from my fingertips to my elbows. The nerves were virtually dead, and the muscles didn't work, so I had no strength or feeling in her limbs. I was a semi-invalid that needed help doing virtually everything.

Mary Lee lovingly cared for me, and we both had to adjust to a new paradigm, where she was the strong one and I was the weak one. This was a new lesson in life for both of us.

Finally, with the help of a skilled and knowledgeable physical therapist, who knew how to stimulate the seemingly dead nerves, he gradually re-activated them. As my feeling began to return, so did my strength, and my muscles began to respond to the signals from the re-awakened nerves. It was a slow process, and because I hadn't been able to walk normally for quite a while, it set up a painful and restricted right hip.

Now, how about a joke with a point . . . a lesson to learn?

There was this highly intelligent donkey, and his owner was extremely proud of him. He asked a friend, "Want to see how smart my donkey is?" His friend replied, "Sure!"

The owner picked up a large two-by-four, swung it back, and smacked that donkey right in the middle of his forehead. His friend cried out, "Why did you do that?!!"

The owner answered, "Well . . . first, I have to get his attention."

During my lifetime, I've come to realize that we're all here on this earth school to learn. I also know that if we don't learn a life lesson we're supposed to learn from a gentle nudging, the stimulus for that lesson will get a little stronger, and more obvious . . . and so on, until we finally get the point and learn that particular lesson.

With many of the physical challenges I've had over the years (shoulder surgery, cancer, brain tumor, severe drug reaction that has ultimately resulted in years of hip pain that still comes and goes, surgery to re-build my face after the accident, gradual loss of my hearing and of my eyesight) the only question I have always asked has been, not "Why, God?" or "Why me?" but rather, "What am I supposed to learn from this?" And my question has always been answered, sometimes immediately, sometimes years later, but I would always eventually realize the answer to my question. Often, it resulted in a deepening of my spiritual faith.

Finally, I began to pray to God, "I'm willing to learn the lessons meant for me, but please, can I sometimes learn through joy and beauty, instead of from pain and suffering?"

Now that I think of it, the life I lived with my Mary Lee was absolutely filled with both of us learning from the joy and beauty in our lives together. Thank you, God!

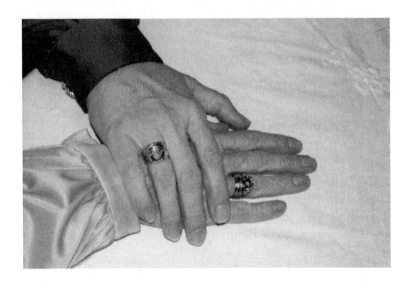

Chapter 7
Fourth Decade—Rainbow Room, Horror, Devotion

Part 1
January 2005 to September 4, 2010

> *"Could I Have This Dance for the Rest of My Life"*
> *"Slow Dancin', Swayin' to the Music"*

THE ANNUAL LESBIAN/GAY DINNER DANCE

We discovered this early October dinner dance sometime in the 1990s and began attending it every year, because it was a fundraiser to fight AIDS, and because it was fun, interesting, and we met many new and old friends there.

Every year, we had our photo taken by a professional photographer who was always there. He began to recognize us each year, and we became friends/acquaintances. His name was David Kirk, of David Kirk Photography in Fort Wayne.

In January, 2000, he was the photographer we chose for our wedding ceremony.

At the 2005 dinner/dance, a young woman took a picture of us dancing, and later came over to our

table and asked if she could interview us. She was a reporter for a publication called *The Rainbow Reader*, and wanted to feature us on the cover and in a long article titled "Two Women—One Journey" for the February (Valentine's Day) issue. She spent time with us that evening and a few days later met us to continue the interview at the YWCA after our workouts with our trainers. She had us read the final article to make sure it was accurate before it was published.

Five years later, she came and spoke briefly at Mary Lee's memorial service.

The picture on the next page was in the center of the article, with two hearts in each corner, and the heading "HAPPY HEARTS FOR 30 YEARS!" and the words to "Could I Have This Dance for the Rest of My Life" framing it.

"The Lady in Red is dancing with me"

"You're Once, Twice, Three Times a Lady"

OUR CARIBBEAN CRUISE

> *"The Wind Beneath My Wings"*
> *"You Raise Me Up"*

30 + 80 AND THEN SOME" PARTY

We'd had a party in our home on our twentieth anniversary, we'd had a formal wedding at our church on our twenty-fifth anniversary, and now, we decided to have a bigger party on our thirtieth anniversary. How-ever, to invite people to drive or fly to a freezing, maybe icy, unpredictable Indiana winter in January didn't seem prudent; so we added the "and then some" to the invitations, and moved it to early spring, in March—and arranged for a much larger venue.

And of course, we all sang together!

Many from *both* of our families came.

MARY LEE'S LOVE OF NATURE
and other joys and talents

Mary Lee would often come home from the university and sit in the swing in our backyard, quietly enjoying the yard and its creatures. We have three bird feeders there. She had a passion for gardening, and even after her physical death, she was still a master gardener, with many of our flowers doubling or even tripling the height they always had through the previous years! Tina once demonstrated the motion she would make over the flowers, and it was as if she was blessing them.

Back in December, 1977, when I was moving from an apartment to my first (and present) home, Mary Lee drove up from Muncie to help. However, when she arrived, she had a fever and chills. She spent the moving time either in my bed, or when they moved that, in her son Joe's bed in her old home. Over the next couple of weeks, she developed a very serious case of pneumonia and later, we realized she should have been in the hospital.

Over the next years, she had pneumonia several more times, and tests finally showed that she had a lung infection (probably contracted from the Oklahoma soil or water where she grew up, and dormant since her childhood.) The name of this group of bacteria is "MAC" (Mycobacterium Avium Complex). She had two respiratory specialists, Dr. Tom Hayhurst, and also Dr. Barbara Nohinek at Lutheran Hospital, who specialized in the treatment of AIDS/lung infections like this by eradicating it with cocktails of heavy-duty antibiotics over a period of time. Eventually, though, those treatments had to cease, because Mary Lee's body couldn't tolerate them.

With the help of Dr. Hayhurst, Mary Lee spent the rest of her life controlling these lung infections and keeping them in check; as soon as she would recognize the early symptoms, she would take specific measures to cut the infection short. After her lungs became more sensitive, we could no longer have a warming, peaceful, and romantic fire in our new Mama Bear fireplace.

We had always enjoyed lighting candles for an occasional romantic dinner, and especially over the holidays, when we would put out our collection of many types and sizes of candles, and light them in whatever room we were in. From our first Christmas together, Mary Lee had brought her love of candles into the new life we shared. Now, we could no longer be in a room with even one lit candle, before she would feel its effect on her lungs. No more Christmas Eve candlelight services at church.

In spite of her wise choices about this situation, during her later years she developed asthma, and she began having to use an inhaler. By then, she was diagnosed with progressive COPD (Chronic Obstructive Pulmonary Disease.)

Dr. Hayhurst was pleased to hear she was singing in my choir; he said it was good therapy for her lungs. She dealt with this long-term physical problem quietly and gracefully, and I never heard her ask, "Why me?" about her lungs. She never complained and was always an unassuming, brave, and strong woman.

2010
One Last Time To Enjoy

Although we didn't know it at the time

> *"Precious and Few Are the Moments We Two Can Share"*
> *"Cherish the Love We Have, cherish the life we live"*

Our last Xena Convention together,
a live concert by Anne Murray or a Celtic Woman show,
our last (and largest) addition to our home,
our last choir concerts and party,
last visits with family and friends,
trips to Shipshewana and to Nashville, IN,
buying (and giving) gifts to each other
last time to have our congregation sing "Happy Anniversary" to us
(as I kiss her on her cheek,)
last family wedding, (Sally Richeson)
our last kiss,
our last hug,
last time to hold hands,
to look into each other's eyes with adoration,
last laugh together,
last cuddle,
last time to harmonize together,
to fall asleep in each other's arms,
to awaken with a smile,
last dance,
and (one of our favorite things . . .)

just doin' stuff together.

EVERYTHING CHANGES

Saturday, July 24, 2010—Sue Errington invited us to a party in her Muncie home, with many of our old N.O.W. friends; we drove down, had a wonderful time, and Mary Lee spent time visiting with Professor Alice Bennett, who was her mentor/advisor while she was working toward her doctorate at Ball State University more than thirty years earlier. On the way home, we noticed how extremely tired we both were, making that trip all in one day.

Later, we discussed the longer drive to Indianapolis we would be making the following Saturday, to attend the annual sight-reading session where we would choose new music for both of our choirs to perform in the new season that fall. The night before we were to leave, Mary Lee said she thought she probably wouldn't go, because her back was hurting more than usual. I begged her to go, so we could share the driving.

Marion, Jill, Sue, Pat and Mary Lee

I said, "I'm afraid I can't make the drive safely by myself." Later that evening, Mary Lee said, "Pat, I'll go with you tomorrow to share the driving." I expressed my appreciation and relief as we went to bed.

On Saturday, July 31, we left early in the morning and switched drivers a few times. We were only about twenty minutes from our destination and had pulled off the interstate so that I could be the one to drive in the heavier traffic in the city.

As was my custom, I reminded Mary Lee to fasten her seat belt, but I was focused on the best way to get to the church and didn't notice that Mary Lee was putting her purse on the floor and hadn't had a chance to buckle her seat belt, as I began to move the car forward . . .

The last thing I remember just at the moment of impact was a fast-moving truck that seemed to come out of nowhere. Weeks later, I checked out the view from each of our vantage points, and because of the overpass, the other driver and I couldn't see each other until it was too late.

Mary Lee and I were both knocked unconscious, and when I finally came to, I looked down and saw that Mary Lee was lying across the seat, with her head in my lap. She had not been able to get her seat belt fastened, and our heads must have collided from the force of the impact of the truck. Emergency workers pried open her door and carefully pulled her unconscious body out and onto a gurney, then put her in an ambulance that headed for the Kokomo Hospital.

Someone told me that they would have to cut me out with the jaws of life. I said, "Okay . . ." and promptly fell unconscious again. I didn't know it until months later when I saw the itemized bills, but at the Kokomo Hospital they ran a lot of tests on me, and determined that my injuries needed to be treated at the Trauma Center in Indianapolis. I became partially conscious as they put me on a helicopter, and all I could think was, "They're taking me away from my Mary Lee, just when she needs me the most!" And then I lost consciousness again.

The next several days were a blur of doctors, nurses, pain, having my left leg propped up on three pillows, near deafness, and being unable to see out of my right eye . . . and every hour, measuring how deeply I could breathe into a tube. They informed me that Mary Lee was sixty miles away, and they bent the rules to put me in touch with her by using their own personal cell phones to call the other hospital. Each time, Mary Lee seemed surprised but very pleased when she heard my voice. Each time, I told her I would call her again, and she said, "Okay." She was released by that hospital the next day, and her son Joe drove her to our home and stayed with her.

Days later, when my sister Margie and her husband Larry were driving me back to our New Haven home, I learned that Mary Lee had suffered a traumatic brain injury and had no short-term memory. She had absolutely *no* memory of any of those phone calls we had shared, and she thought that after thirty-six years together, I had deserted her! I was shocked and dismayed to learn this.

The next day, Barb Werling, a dear friend who was in both of my choirs, drove me to my family doctor, who agreed with Barb's advice that I needed to see my Mary Lee in person every day, to help her to gradually realize that I was there, and that I would spend time with her every day from now on, so she would have confidence that I would be there with her.

I asked Joe to take me to the hospital where she was having three days of tests to determine if a rehabilitation facility might help to heal her brain trauma. Soon, he pushed my wheelchair into her room and to the far side of her bed, where I asked the nurse to lower the railing on that side. I stood up and gingerly crawled up onto the bed with her, took her hand, and talked softly to her.

She gently touched my face and said, "Your face looks awful!"

I replied that they were going to operate on it in a few days to rebuild that side of my face, and that it would get better.

The nurse who had watched all of this smiled and said, "You must be Pat. She's been asking for you."

I even gave her a calendar, with the days marked that I would be coming to see her every day . . . except for the Monday that a surgeon would be operating on my face in Indianapolis.

While she was in rehab, if she told a nurse I hadn't been there for two weeks, the nurse would show her the calendar and point to the day before and how it was marked that I'd been there, and would be coming to see her each day. I enlisted choir members, other friends, family, and neighbors to drive me there each day to visit her and share a meal. We were both so seriously injured that neither of us had an appetite, and we encouraged each other to have some healthy nourishment each day. Once there, my current driver would borrow a wheelchair for me, and the three of us would share lunch time and try to stay long enough to encourage Mary Lee during one of her many therapy sessions, before my pain got so intense that I needed to be taken back home to lie in bed for the rest of the day.

After two-and-a-half weeks, they told me that she was working hard and progressing well, but that Medicare's time limit to pay was only for three weeks. They checked and found they could transfer her to a New Haven rehab very near our home. I no longer had to depend on others to drive me to her; it was so nearby that I could drive there (very carefully) in about five minutes, rather than the thirty-minute trip to the hospital rehab. Now, I could be with her for ten or eleven hours and share two meals with her every day. However, it was still very distressing to her when I had to leave each evening to go back home. She kept phoning me at home, pleading with me to stay there with her, or to bring her home with me.

During those five weeks, Mary Lee and I had each been working hard to recover from the accident—she, in the rehab facility for the traumatic brain injury, and I at home, after extensive facial surgery, five broken ribs, and a deep leg wound with a serious burn on top of it. It was slow, but we were both making progress, and we looked forward to being together once again in our home.

They also encouraged me to take her out for small trips; I took her to have lunch with friends, have her hair done by Arlene, our long-time hairdresser, take her to church the following Sunday, and make a couple of field trips to our home.

It was the first time in over a month that we were together in our home, so I showed her the rainbow room, which had been completed just three months before the accident. She didn't remember it at all, so it was a wonderful surprise to her.

We went into our new miracle Rainbow Room. She had named it that, months earlier, because each wall was a different pastel color: blue, green, yellow, and pink, with the white doors and woodwork we had painted. Each of the six file cabinets, all containing choir music, was a different primary color: red, green, yellow, blue, plus silver, and gold.

She had no memory of the construction of that room during the previous five months, with all the finishing work we had done after the builders had completed their work. We had been painting, staining, purchasing shelves, building three bookcases, and moving some of the furniture from other rooms of our home into that new room. We had literally transformed almost all of the other rooms by reclaiming them from junk-filled chaos, with bags and boxes of choir supplies and file cabinets stored in every room throughout the house and also in the garage. For the past several years, we had both been quite discouraged by the mess and had finally decided to add on what would become the largest room in our home, where we could then gather up *all* of the choir items and furniture into that one room and its closet.

I played the silly rainbow-colored chicken for her, complete with music and a confused dance which made her laugh. She had given it to me the previous winter, when I was recovering from a painful operation on my legs, and I had needed a laugh, too. She had surprised me with it as I lay on the bed, crying from the unrelenting pain, in hopes of giving me a smile. Instead, it had made me outright laugh!

The new room was an incredibly exciting project, and from the very beginning of our planning, we affirmed that everything about it would be done in Divine Order, from the construction company we chose, to the workers, to our choices of how it would look and what to buy to complete it.

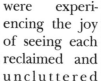

On this day, it was as if she were experiencing the joy of seeing each reclaimed and uncluttered room for the first time, and she was incredibly pleased as I pushed her wheelchair into each area of our home.

She shed a few tears of joy, when she saw how nice the family room looked, with all the boxes and bags of choir stuff gone. I pushed her wheelchair around to each room, to show her how vastly improved it looked from how she remembered it.

We toured the living room, which now had a beautiful couch, instead of the large, messy desk piled high with choir papers which had dominated that room for years.

Then, she saw the soft light and the beautiful transformation in her lapidary room, where she had often worked to plan, cut, form, polish, and design many different kinds of beautiful jewelry for friends and family over the many years that we've lived here. Previously, there had been three large, dirty file cabinets full of music, and a cart stacked high with boxes of choir things that had dominated that room. On that Saturday in September, she expressed enthusiasm about creating more jewelry there soon, since the room was now more inviting and beautiful.

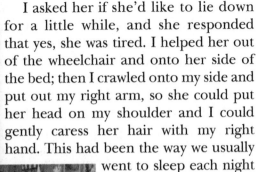

Family Room

We took a brief look into her small bedroom, where she often sat in her favorite chair and read, or watched DVDs of *Xena, Warrior Princess* TV shows, or took light naps. The pillow on her chair read, "a woman's place is in the house and . . . the senate!"

She laughed at the clutter on her bed, and I told her that the stacks of card on the end of her bed were all the many get well cards for her that we'd been receiving every day. After sharing each one with her when I visited her, I'd deposit them there.

Then we went across the hall to our much larger bedroom, and as we looked out the large bay window, she said

Living Room

that all the plants on the windowsill were looking good and healthy.

Mary Lee had always been the one who had taken such good care of the plants, both indoors and outside. She dearly loved working in the garden. When she first began living here in 1978, she gradually transformed the yards surrounding our home (front, back, and sides) with many beautiful flowers, bushes, and trees.

I asked her if she'd like to lie down for a little while, and she responded that yes, she was tired. I helped her out of the wheelchair and onto her side of the bed; then I crawled onto my side and put out my right arm, so she could put her head on my shoulder and I could gently caress her hair with my right hand. This had been the way we usually went to sleep each night in the past. Within minutes, we were both sound asleep. That short but very sweet nap was the only time in almost five weeks that we'd been able to fall asleep together. We didn't know that it would also be our last time. When we awoke, it was time to take her back to rehab, and I stayed there with her until I had to drive back home before it was dark. I was still somewhat nervous about driving.

On the last Sunday in August, I had picked her up at rehab so that we could go to our church service together. We were both still somewhat fragile physically, but it was wonderful to be in the midst of all that love and support from our many friends, and once again to be sitting in our regular pew, with my arm around her shoulders.

When our minister got up to give her message, I was surprised that Mary Lee shifted so that her back was toward me, but then she nestled into my body and relaxed. We both relaxed, enjoying our loving closeness as we listened to the minister.

That following Friday and especially Saturday, Mary Lee and I had wonderful, beautiful days together. We took more short trips, and on Saturday we paid a three-hour visit to our home and shared a supper at our kitchen table. The rainbow

The Lapidary

room was again a wonderful surprise for her, and she asked me to push her wheelchair slowly around the room as I told her about it.

After a while, she said she was tired and needed to get back to rehab soon. She had been on oxygen for the past two days, but she still seemed to be doing much, much better than earlier. She had recently been improving so much that her regular personality, her intelligent strength, her delightful sense of humor, and her affectionate love for me had all been becoming gradually once again more evident, especially as I had recently been witnessing her interactions with her occupational, speech, and physical therapists, as well as with the nurses and aides. She also didn't seem to be having the short-term memory loss or confusion that had been so evident during the previous weeks.

While there that Saturday, I laid out some clothes for the aide to help her put on the next morning, because we planned to make our second trip to our church. We were both continuing to heal very gradually.

As I was leaving to return home that evening, I remarked to one of her main nurses, "I think I'm getting my Mary Lee back. She might be coming home soon!"

After I arrived home that evening, I phoned her and told her how much I was looking forward to tomorrow. She answered that she was excited about it, too. We said, "Goodnight, honey, I'll see you tomorrow," and "I love you," and both of us went to bed and slept.

Part 2

September 5, 2010 to the present day
THE END - OR NOT?

At 2:50 am, I was awakened by the ringing of my bedside phone. A nurse at rehab said that Mary Lee had just had a stroke (she couldn't move one side and couldn't talk) and that her heart had stopped. They were attempting to get it started, and the hospital ambulance was on its way.

I immediately called Joe, Mary Lee's son, and told him I'd meet him at the hospital; then I called Jannie, her daughter in California, so she could book a flight to come here. Finally, I called Rev. Mary Wood, our minister, made a copy of her living will, and drove to the ER, where Joe came in soon after. The doctor told us that her heart had been stopped for quite a number of minutes. They had given her CPR at the rehab facility and also in the ambulance. He said that because of all that time, she would probably have brain damage, even if they now used heroic efforts to revive her. Joe and I immediately agreed with her living will that she wouldn't have wanted to "live" like that.

As I entered where Mary Lee lay, I kissed her on the lips and held her hand as I gently rubbed my thumb across the back of it. As I stroked her hair, I said softly to her as I looked up above us, "I'm not sure where you are right now, but I know you're here, and I know you can hear me."

I had good reason to think that she was probably fighting to stay here for my sake, so I said to her, "I don't know what I'll do without you, but I'll be okay. I don't want you to fight the process that you're going through right now, in order to try to stay here with me. You have a very special journey you'll be taking, and I want you to go gently and peacefully, and I release you to go to your next place."

Over the past few years, she had always presumed she would be the first to die, because she was several years older than I. But anytime she ever tried to talk to me about "after I'm gone..." I would immediately hold up my hand to stop what she was starting to tell me, and I would say to her, "I can't even bear to think about living without you . . . it's too painful!"

I would never let her talk about it, and her attempts to say anything about her eventual death would always bring me to tears.

Then, some months before the accident, she had asked me three questions:

1. "Do you believe love is eternal?"

I answered, "Yes, absolutely; I believe it's one of the few things that's eternal."

2. "Do you think we'll be together again?"

I said, "Yes, that's what soulmates do; we'll either be together in another body and in another lifetime, or we'll be together in the spirit world, with God."

3. "Will we be in touch?"

I was less certain about this, but I answered, "I think we probably will, somehow."

Now, here in the hospital, I reminded her of those questions she had previously asked me, and my answers to each one, and that we would be forever connected by our love.

> *"You Know You Love Her When You Let Her Go"*

Then Joe came to the other side of her bed and said his final goodbyes to his mother.

Rev. Mary Wood had come in sometime during all of this and stood there, quietly observing.

I don't remember if I kissed her again before we left the room a few minutes later.

After they pronounced her dead, they handed *Joe* the death certificate to sign, as next of kin. I had a Durable Power of Attorney, previously signed by Mary Lee in 1994, and I said to them, "She was my life partner for thirty-six years. I should be the one to sign that."

They informed me that Indiana law says that it has to be a blood relative that signs it. In my shock and grief, I found that our homophobic state legislature had ignored and nullified both my place in her life and also our thirty-six-year relationship, as if neither existed or mattered. Later, I wondered how many other loving couples they'd hurt this way.*

The next day at the funeral home, the same thing happened, with a form giving permission for her cremation having to be signed, again by a blood relative!

I told them that back in 1983, when Mary Lee and I had both obtained pre-paid funerals, we had decided then that cremation would be a part of our future funeral plans, and that Joe knew nothing about it. Talk about adding gross insult to grievous injury!

And now, on October 6, 2014, just over four years later, this will no longer happen to other loving couples, since now Indiana (and twenty-nine other states, so far) finally has legal marriage and all of its rights, protection and recognition, so long denied to us! Wow!

* on June 26, 2015, the Supreme Court ruled that States cannot keep same-sex couples from marrying and must recognize their unions.

But wait, was this really the end of our incredible relationship? Nu-uh. That's not the way soulmates do it—at least, not Mary Lee and Pat.

But . . . what about our relationship? As Missy Good, one of our friends and a writer for the TV series, *Xena, Warrior Princess* had declared at one of the annual Xena conventions in California, "There were three main characters in all of these stories: Xena, Gabrielle . . . and their relationship. Each of the three was equally important."

And so it was with us . . .

Saturday, September 11, 2010—Held her memorial service at Unity, our church. Sent Thank You notes for flowers and donations made in Mary Lee's name.

Sent out to friends and family over a hundred copies of Christmas cards she had painted, along with a photo of us (see the cover of our book) and also with some of the things I'd written about her, and a copy of her obituary, for those out of town or out of state.

December 6, 2010—Jannie and I visited Tina Zion for the first time. It took me three months to work up the courage to go meet Tina.

December 30—The eastern part of my family came for Christmas

For the next two years (and then some) I served as Mary Lee's executor: I filed *many* signed legal papers with the Allen County Auditor, set up a new checking account in ML's name in order to pay any outstanding bills and debts.

I wrote checks for all final medical payments. This took many months, there were so many—and almost all were out of town.

I filed four kinds of taxes for her: 2010 and 2011, Estate/Trust, and Inheritance; paid all taxes; began to

---

> *"Honey, I Miss You"*
> *"I Couldn't Live Without Your Love"*
> *"I Would Give Anything I Own . . . just to have you back again"*
> *"Gone Too Soon"*

distribute some of Mary Lee's things, first to family and friends, donated much of her clothing to needy women's groups that we both had supported for years.

Stopped all of her many magazine subscriptions

Paid monetary donations to organizations which Mary Lee had supported for years. Eventually, distributed all inheritance monies to designated beneficiaries

Beginning in 2011 I honored our home and yard by having improvements made, most of which we had already decided earlier to do or to have done.

Sometime in 2011—Mary Lee began "sending" me songs with messages and encouragement.

July, 2011—Embarked on a trip to Nevada to visit with family members in small groups; got to know them better and also shared more about Mary Lee with each of them.

September 2012—Cleaned out and packed up eight very large boxes of Xena memorabilia and shipped to California.

I attended the February 2012 Xena Convention. I gave away free to the fans Xena memorabilia, from mugs to jewelry, DVDs, CDs, VHS videotapes, luggage, clothing—including many t-shirts, sweaters, jackets (silk and leather), fan fiction, posters, albums of photos, and several things I had written about Mary Lee. People seemed hungry to know about us and it seemed that many had observed us at the conventions. A couple of people told me they wished they could get to know us, but didn't want to intrude. We were completely unaware of this dynamic, and I regretted that we didnt get to know some of them.

William Shatner and a film crew were interviewing myriads of people for a documentary they were making about the final Xena Convention and the TV show and what it meant to them. They interviewed the organizers, many of the actors in the show, and people who had come to the conventions multiple times. A couple of friends took pictures of William interviewing me.

I began to say my goodbyes to our many friends there.

I made a statement to the whole convention about her—and that she is still very alive, and continues to be very active in my life.

With William Shatner

AN EARLY E-MAIL TO A XENA FRIEND

Sharon, this is to let *you* know that I'm doing better and better as I learn more about another whole world of existence, and that those souls who've left behind their bodies from this life are still very much alive in another place.

1. I'm working at really developing the "right side" (the creative and "being" side) of my brain, with much deeper meditation and much more quiet time and less time spent with the left side of my brain (doing and thinking.)

I had a strong faith, but I was pretty illiterate and uninformed about the spirits in the afterlife and what they could do and what sapped their energy. I'm learning to be much more sensitive to recognizing my Murdy's communications with me, which I'm slowly realizing are pretty often—I just hadn't been aware of them or sensitive to them. I sound like I've gone "off the deep end," but I assure you, it *is* real—and when I thought (twice) that she had left me and wasn't going to return, I was afraid, helpless, falling into a hopeless depression, and overcome by loneliness. I found that I didn't have the "spirit facts" or knowledge. When I slowly became more informed, I had a peace come over me and knew she was here with me all the time, but just *sometimes* was interacting with me. Just as she was learning the ropes

Sharon Delaney and Adam Malin organized all the Xena conventions

on the "other side," I've been learning on this side. As she told me recently, "we're *both* learning to do it better."

2. I'm the person who's in charge of her "Revocable Living Trust" and am also the executor of her "Last Will and Testament," so there have been *lots* of legal stuff to do these past several months, and belongings to disseminate to her family and friends, 4 sets of taxes to prepare for filing, clothes to donate to women at the homeless shelter and "women in transition," for women who need professional clothes to apply for better jobs after more education and training.

3. I'm learning to live a different kind of life without her being with me *physically,* but still having her spirit, with me, with her same personality, sense of humor, intelligence, kindness and incredible love.

4. My family and friends have been incredibly supportive as I journey through these changes, with occasional "waves of grief" washing over me at unexpected times, and I'm doing more things with others and I'm also learning to live and laugh and enjoy my life, however it continues to unfold.

5. I've learned that a lot of my "processing the grief" comes at times with a lot of my "jabbering" to friends. And it seems that I've been jabbering much more than usual in this letter. Thanks for listening.

My statement for Xena fans and friends at the 2012 Convention:

(written in 2011, but not presented until the following year)

Dear Xena fans and friends,

If you recall some of the "audacious" fun Mary Lee and Pat have had at these conventions, since our 1st one in 2001 . . . like the "Hollywood kiss" I gave an unsuspecting Mary Lee in 2009, in front of the "Bitch Slap" panel (including Renée in her nun's costume) or our comment to Allison a few years ago about her famous line, "Now we know who we are . . . we're THESPIANS!"

These conventions have been the highlight of our years, with new and old friends, the fans and the stars, all supporting our love and fun, in a way that made us feel validated and cherished, and even like "role models" in our thirty-six-year-long loving and rewarding relationship. Xena and Gabrielle taught us about being "soul mates" and we know that we ARE, just as many of you are.

Many of you had believed, along with us, that in that last scene of the last episode of Season Six, when Xena and Gabrielle were talking together at the railing of the ship (with Gabrielle holding the urn with Xena's ashes) . . . and then you saw that Gabby was ALONE at the railing—you may have also reacted as we did, saying, "Now, that's just pitiful*; Gabrielle has gone 'round the bend, she's deluded by her grief, she's imagining something that is NOT true, is not reality. What an AWFUL way to bring this wonderful series to a close!*

Well, last summer Mary Lee and I were both very seriously hurt in a violent truck/car crash, and more than a month later, Mary Lee died from complications. I went to the hospital and talked to her, held her hand, kissed her, and told her NOT to try to stay here for my sake, but to peacefully continue her journey to her "next place." During the previous year, we had already talked about love being eternal, that we'd see each other again, and that we'd be forever connected by our love. Then I kissed her and told her I loved her.

Beginning the next day, Mary Lee's soul connected with me often . . . in a dream, a butterfly that wouldn't leave, a bird, a bunny (each of whom responded to what I said) and I found that her intelligence, personality, love for me, and her sense of humor were all still intact, and that she was even stronger, without that injured, eighty-five-year-old human body to hold her back.

And so, I found out that the writers of that last episode—and Gabrielle—were not "crazy" or "deluded."

THEY WERE RIGHT—that LOVE—and the SOUL—ARE ETERNAL, and that souls don't have to be separated—even in "death!"

My best wishes to you all. Have a wonderful conference!

With much love, Pat Deihl, Soulmate of Dr. Mary Lee Richeson.

By the way, I've asked Mary Lee if she'll be here with me, and she assured me that of course she will, and furthermore, anyone I hug or who hugs me, she'll be hugging, too.

I felt Mary Lee's presence on my right side, and I turned to her and said, "Look, they're making a wave and giving us a standing ovation!"

Friends and strangers came up to me later, some in tears, many thanking me for giving them hope that when a loved one dies, it doesn't have to be over for them.

People I hadn't known shared with me their own stories of loved ones who had passed on, letting them know (often in unique ways) that they were there, and that they were okay.

A couple from Dallas on the plane, a man in the swimming pool in the hotel, a young woman who had recently lost a loved one—they all were touched by my story, and have asked me to let them know when this book is published, so they can buy it and read it.

Many people are not just curious, but they're hungering to learn more about all this . . . I certainly didn't set out to be a missionary or a teacher—but if what I am now writing in the second half of this book helps ease a burden of pain, fear, or grief in any reader, I am pleased for them.

"Take what you can use, and just leave the rest." I'm not here to persuade or convince anyone of anything; I'm merely sharing my own experiences.

OUR FINAL DINNER/DANCE PICTURE

In October, 2009, David, our favorite photographer, met us as we were approaching the entrance and told us he was helping with the large auction that year and wouldn't be taking the professional pictures. When he saw our look of disappointment, he reached into his pocket and said, "But I have my camera; would you like me to take your picture?" We eagerly agreed, and as he took our picture, he said he would send it to us by e-mail. We hadn't thought about the fact that he didn't know our e-mail address, and all three of us simply forgot about it . . .

Eleven months later, when David saw Mary Lee's obituary in the newspaper, he sent me a sympathy card, and I remembered about the picture he had taken the previous October. I called him and asked if by chance he still had that picture, and he said, "Yes, I do; give me your e-mail address, and I'll send it to you."

When it arrived as an attachment on an e-mail from him, I couldn't open it at first. I didn't remember how we looked or what we were wearing, and her death was so recent (less than a month) that I was afraid to see it. When I finally opened the attachment and saw it, I wept, because I thought it was one of the best pictures we'd ever had taken. You could see the excitement and anticipation in our facial expressions, and even our posture, as we were looking forward to enjoying another dinner dance together.

"Never Gonna Dance Again, the Way I Danced With You"

Is it any wonder that we've chosen David's picture for the cover of our book? Mary Lee had never seen it before her death, but now she has seen it, and she likes it, too.

OUR PROFESSIONAL PORTRAIT

The year after Mary Lee's death, I made a long distance phone call and commissioned a large oil painting to be created by my incredibly talented artist/brother, Charles Deihl ("Bud"). In our letters and discussions on the phone, since we had so many activities and interests we loved (I sent him sixty photos to possibly use in the background) he invented a memory border, with twenty-one smaller paintings, each one depicting many of our interests and passions in life: hers, mine, and ours.

The finished portrait, with a light he provided when he drove six hours to our home to install it, now hangs in the center of our living room wall, right above the couch. It is the first thing visitors see when they enter the front door, a commanding and beautiful presence.

> *"I Know I'll Never Find Another You"*

THE LOVE SONG COMPOSED FOR US

Larry Heral, a talented and inspiring composer/performer at Unity, offered to compose a song for the highest bidder during a church fundraiser/silent auction several years ago. The ever-tenacious bulldog, I just kept going back to the bidding form and finally won the bid.

I told Larry I'd like him to write a love song from me for Mary Lee, and that there was no rush. He was a very busy musician, along with his wife, Lisa. He asked me several times if I was ready for the interview which would give him some ideas for the song (style, text, rhythm, etc.) and I kept replying, "Not yet; we're working through some things right now." If you've wondered whether our wonderful, loving relationship was always perfect . . . nu-uh.

We always worked it out, but yes, there were occasional rough spots along the way for us two strong, independent, intelligent but sometimes irrational women who dearly loved each other.

Anyway, I waited too long, and the accident happened, and five weeks later, Mary Lee's death and my grief came. Several months after her passing, I told Larry that now I was finally ready, except that it will be a love song for both of us while we are living on two separate planes of existence. Larry came to our home and sat on the couch beneath our portrait, which I explained to him in detail. He asked me to talk about our lives together and to share some memories.

During our talk, he shared a very personal story about how he had always been very narrow-minded about gays and lesbians and their lifestyle. But he said that over a long period of time, he had observed us in church as we sat quietly every week, showing each other a kind respect, sensitive emotional support, joy, and a kind of love that didn't call attention to us but gently radiated out from us. He told me that because of us, and the kind of love we obviously shared, he had come to the conclusion that "it's only love, and there's nothing wrong with that." I was stunned when he told me that our example (without our realizing it) had completely changed his mind about the homophobia which he no longer had.

Some people may think that "homophobia" means a *fear* of homosexuals but Webster defines it as "an extreme and irrational aversion to or antipathy toward homosexual people." The Oxford Dictionary defines it as "dislike of or prejudice against homosexual people."

About the same time, another man, also a dear friend from Unity, had privately shared a similar story with me, that witnessing Mary Lee's and my relationship had also changed his heart about the same thing. I feel very humble; we never sought to teach anyone anything; we just simply cherished each other.

Some weeks later, Larry and Lisa came to my home and Larry lifted his guitar, played and sang the song he had just completed, to see if I approved of it. He gave me a sheet with the words and played it again.

It brought me to tears, and I told him it was so much *more* than I had expected, because it wasn't just a love song, it was a sweet and powerful tribute to our relationship!

He told me that what inspired him to write those words to the song was the very large oil portrait of us, painted for me by my brother Bud, with its memory border of twenty-one smaller paintings, each one depicting many of our interests and joys in life.

Larry made the first verse of the song about Mary Lee's art, the second verse about my music, and the whole song is about our relationship.

" . . . and we were meant to be."

> ## "Masterpiece —Mary Lee and Pat"

As I look back . . . there is no past,
I see instead what we created.
A work of art . . . inspired by hearts
entwined in love and boldly stated.

A masterpiece of love, laid out for all to see,
Colored outside the lines, unbound . . . fearlessly
Each shade expressing all that we were meant to be,
and we were meant to be.

Two melodies . . . soon came to be . . . a symphony
of love unfolding
Right from the start . . . two trusting hearts
sang out the song they'd been withholding

A masterpiece of love played out for all to hear,
Composed, refined, perfected through the passing years.
Each note expressing all that we were meant to be.
and we were meant to be.

We've been as one . . . in all we've done
Against all odds we stood together
Tested and proved . . . all doubt removed
I know we're bound in love forever!

As I look back . . . there is no past,
I see instead what we created.
A work of art . . . inspired by hearts
entwined in love and boldly stated.

A masterpiece of love, laid out for all to see,
Colored outside the lines, unbound . . . fearlessly
Each shade expressing all that we were meant to be,

and we were meant to be,
We were meant to be . . .
We were meant to be!

A SPECIAL MOMENT WITH THAT SONG

On January 17, 2014 (two days after Mary Lee's birthday) I was in the Rainbow Room, preparing to burn a CD of this song which Larry had written for us. I turned on the sound system, including the left speaker, which has this small sign on top of it: "Those who sing . . . Pray twice," and I plugged my small recorder into the CD burner, so it would play through the speakers. I had recorded our song at a live concert which was Larry's first public performance of it.

I successfully made a CD of it and shed tears several times as I played it back, since the words are so touching to me and so descriptive of us. I turned off the small recorder, ejected the new CD, and turned off the power strip as I rose from my chair. I turned around as I headed over to turn off the left speaker . . . and sobbed and laughed when I saw that the sign on the speaker had definitely been moved 90 degrees by . . . guess who? I realized that Mary Lee had been listening to it, too. She wanted me to know that she'd heard it along with me, and she was also touched by it.

Since that time, she *has* interacted with me in several different ways, but now, I never expect it— it always surprises and delights me . . . and I always thank her and tell her I love her . . . and what a miracle she continues to be for me!

EARLY ON, SOME VERY ROUGH TIMES!

> *"Too Soon Gone"*

Although Mary Lee had been interacting with me from the first day after her death and seemed to have rescued me from the deep, torturous grief, the hopelessness and depression I had always greatly feared during our years together, during those first three months, there were two long periods that I thought she was gone for good. I would try to talk to her, but she never responded in any way, and I felt . . . abandoned.

During both of these extended periods I was thrust into a depression of emotional fragility, and instead of reaching out to friends and family, I curled up inside myself, unable to converse with others, and always on the verge of tears, which spilled out often. I couldn't think clearly and kept losing things that were important to have at hand. I was emotionally unstable and unable to cope with anything or anyone. The peace that passes understanding was gone, and all I could see in my future was chaos and disorder and desolate loneliness. I sought order by constantly doing, doing, doing things that needed to be done, from the time I awoke each day and into the wee hours of the night . . . or early morning.

Early one evening, I felt so lonely in our large and empty home, I called my sister Margie (who now goes by Margaret, but I've always called her by the name she had when we were young kids,) who was still working at the business she and Larry own. I asked if I could come there to be with her because I couldn't stand the quiet of the empty house. She said, "Of course!" I took along some work I needed to do (I don't remember what) and we sat together and I talked non-stop for a very long time, while she listened patiently to me. Finally, I asked her which of the two desks she was using and asked if I could use the other one. We sat with our backs to each other, both concentrating on the work at hand. I was okay, because I didn't feel so alone while I was with her. I felt as if her quiet, caring attention, her emotional support had rescued me from an intolerable situation. My love and appreciation for my youngest sister have continued and grown since that evening four years ago.

SOME "WHAT IF's" and "IF ONLY's"

Whenever one of us came home, we would call out "I'm home!" to the other one. One day, I went toward her room calling out to her, and we were both startled, because she had been taking a nap in her chair. I determined I wouldn't awaken her that way anymore, so I stopped calling out to her when I arrived home. And she began to do the same. We often didn't know when the other one had arrived, or how long they'd been home and doing things. I regret that we lost that enthusiastic greeting to each other. Now, I wish I could call out to her and have her come in and give me a hug. It was a little thing, but I came to miss it, and I think she did, too.

"I Should Have Brought You Flowers"

There were times I was brusque and insensitive in things I said or did, and oblivious to moments when she was hurt by this. Because we knew each other so well, sometimes we took it for granted that we knew what the other one was thinking . . . and sometimes we were so wrong!

Once, Mary Lee came from her bedroom into the family room and sadly said to me, "I miss you!" I had been spending a lot of time working on things for the choirs, and I realized she was feeling like a choir widow. Immediately, I took her into my arms and onto my lap, held her, and paid attention only to her. But eventually, I would become preoccupied with choir matters again. I'm a good choir director, but too often, I was not a close enough companion to her.

Sometimes Mary Lee would tell me that she missed that strong passion of our courting days, and I usually responded that now, we had more of a steady and deeply committed love, without the frenzied lives we used to live, always trying to be together. Now, I would give anything to be able to show her the passion she desired.

Indeed, we had countless precious moments together, but I couldn't let myself even consider that she might not be here in the future. It was too painful for me to contemplate, so I refused to think about or to even let her talk about it.

"I Always Thought That I'd See You Again"

I wish I had been more patient and understanding all the time, not just most of the time.

More recently, I've said to Mary Lee that I want my soul to continue to learn and mature while I'm living this life, so that I'll do even better in the next lifetime I hope we'll have together.

PAT'S CONTINUING GOALS

Continue to get to know my family members and good friends better and to learn to be more *present* whenever I'm with them.

Take every opportunity presented to experience my own spiritual growth, to learn everything I can about things of the spirit.

Each morning, affirm Divine Order in my life, and live that way moment by moment, more and more.

Continue to learn to live my life in a new way, without my soul-mate's physical presence in this world.

Learn to find my own joy in my life, and to express thankfulness daily.

My desire is to learn to live my life by this adage I once heard:

"Life is better when you are happy . . . But life is best when other people are happy because of you."

Artwork by Kara Tobin

Chapter 8
A New Beginning—Butterflies, Birds, and Bunnies

My "new" life, without Mary Lee's physical presence

> *"Unforgettable"*
> *"So Far Away"*

The day that I released my Mary Lee at the hospital to begin her transition was shortly before four a.m. on Sunday, September 5, 2010. When I returned home, instead of going to bed, I composed and sent an e-mail to both of our families and many friends, to tell what had just happened. Then, instead of lying down to rest, I got dressed and went to our church (Unity Christ Church,) where I knew I would get loving support from all our dear friends there.

Our minister had already told everyone before I arrived that Mary Lee had passed on only hours earlier. What a gamut of loving hugs and words of support as I walked through the narthex and into the sanctuary toward our pew. It gave me a peace and courage I wouldn't have thought possible!

My first shock of grieving reality hit early in the service. Since it was the first Sunday of the month, we sang "Happy Birthday" and then "Happy Anniversary" to those in the congregation who would be celebrating that special day during this month, and I suddenly realized that when January came, they would no longer be singing "Happy Birthday" to my Mary Lee or "Happy Anniversary" to both of us as we went up in front. It was the first of many chilling realizations I would be experiencing for many months to come. I said nothing to anyone about it, but I suffered a stab of pain in my heart.

That afternoon, Joe and I went to retrieve all of Mary Lee's things from the Rehabilitation Center where she'd been staying, and I brought them all home. I did a laundry and hung her clean clothes in her closet. I unpacked her bag and put each of her things in their usual place; I didn't go to bed until late that evening, when I was exhausted.

Jan had flown in from her home in California, and she and her brother Joe came over late on Monday morning. The three of us spent hours composing her obituary, each of us becoming increasingly amazed at the abundance and scope of her many interests, accomplishments, and honors throughout her life. At one point, Jan looked inconsolable, and Joe asked her what was going on. She answered, "I'll never be able to live up to her." Joe answered, "Jan, no one could live up to her."

MARY LEE'S OBITUARY

Mary Lee Richeson was born Mary Lee Radebaugh, daughter of Leroy and Grace Radebaugh, January 15th 1925, in Henryetta Oklahoma. As a small child, she delivered bottles of milk for the family dairy. As the Great Depression hit, the family was impoverished and scattered for a while. Life was difficult, and for a year her education was interrupted due to family circumstances and illness.

She developed a love of literature and science, graduating Salutatorian from Henryetta High School class of 1944. With the help of her grandmother she relocated to northern California and worked a series of menial jobs to finance her education at San Jose State University, from which she graduated Magnum Cum Laude in 1948. She was granted a Master of Arts from Stanford University in 1949, and returned to San Jose State as an earth science instructor for several years.

In 1947 she married William Richeson, also from Henryetta. Together they had two children, Jan Elizabeth in 1953, and Joseph William in 1954.

She moved from California to Fort Wayne, Indiana in 1956. During these years she held leadership positions in the PTA, and did a lot of volunteer demonstrations for science and biology in public schools. Mary Lee was politically active working for John F. Kennedy, Robert Kennedy, J. Edward Roush, and Birch Bayh.

She held teaching positions at St. Francis College and Indiana Institute of Technology. In 1978, she received an Ed.D. from Ball State University and was shortly thereafter employed as a biology instructor at Indiana-Purdue University at Fort Wayne. She retired as Professor Emeritus in 1994.

She is remembered at IPFW in the Marthe Rosenfeld/Mary Lee Richeson Women's Studies scholarship, awarded annually.

She served as a member and local president of the National Organization for Women, and has been a contributing member of YWCA, Planned Parenthood, Charis House, The Feminist Majority, and Emily's List. Mary Lee also has been a long time supporter of Representative Jill Long, Senator Hillary Clinton, and is a current supporter of Dr. Tom Hayhurst.

In 1975 she met Pat Deihl who became her life partner, sharing love of vocal music, (and Xena!). Since 1978, they have shared a home at their current location in New Haven, Indiana. The home has been expanded three times, including a music room just completed early this summer.

Mary Lee was a firm believer in the eternal power of love, a belief that influenced a great many people over the years, including Reverend Gregory Guice. She became very close to the current pastor of Unity Christ Church, Reverend Mary Wood.

Mary Lee held a reverence and love of life, nature, science, and the arts. She is a founding member of Acres, and a continuing contributor to National Wildlife Federation and a past member of the Isaac Walton League.

For years, she has had a love of the arts, collecting music of many types, including everything from opera to pop. She frequently took her children to concerts. She was a long time member of the Unity Christ Church choir, and of the Celebration Singers and the Festival Choir (the musical arm of Associated Churches) where she sang alto. She actively supported her children and grandchildren in pursuit of the arts as well.

In the last two decades she has been a very ardent fan of *Xena Warrior Princess*, attending conventions, where she and Pat became popular fixtures and role models.

Since her heart attack in 1998, she has worked hard with personal trainers, especially her beloved Sue Bair to sustain health, strength, and vigor of life.

Mary Lee has been a practicing artist in stone jewelry and lapidary since the early 1960s until the present, and has a room dedicated to that in her home. In addition she has created artworks in oil and acrylics paints and since 1998 has created her own Christmas and greeting cards, often treasured by the recipients in collections.

Surviving are Life Partner of 36 years Pat Deihl, Children Joe Richeson of Fort Wayne, Indiana, Jan Davis of Corona, California, and Grandchildren Paul Richeson, Sally Cates, Katie Davis, and Julie Davis.

Preceding her in death were her father Leroy Radebaugh, mother Grace Radebaugh, brothers Theon Radebaugh, Tommy Radebaugh, and sister Eula Mae Payne.

Memorials preferred to
Mary Lee Richeson Scholarship c/o women's studies department Indiana-Purdue University, Fort Wayne or to Unity Christ Church.

Calling is from 2 to 4 and 6 to 8 pm Thursday, Sept. 9, 2010, at E. Harper & Son Funeral Home, New Haven. She will be laid to rest in Greenlawn Memorial Park. A Celebration of Life service is 3 pm Saturday, Sept. 11, 2010 at Unity Christ Church, 3232 Crescent Ave., Fort Wayne.

Some additional remarks from Pat:

Her bravery and determination were stunning, as she and Pat fought intensely for over five weeks to overcome and be healed from a serious car accident.

She had to get used to hearing Pat say "I came alive in '75!" She brought great love, joy, fun, love of life, learning, and a deeper faith to Pat and now, her soul is continuing to learn—and still teaches Pat—from the other side. I love you, Murdy!

When we completed our work, I picked out the clothing and jewelry she would be wearing for the viewing at the funeral home. We spent several hours there, going over all that would be done and how much each thing would cost. I was still in shock from losing her, but I became very incensed when they said that Indiana law decreed that I couldn't sign some of the legal papers, because I wasn't a blood relative. Joe signed them, instead.

On Tuesday morning, I awoke from what I thought was an incredibly loving but brief dream: we were standing at the foot of our bed, both dressed in winter pajamas and just holding each other, in a firm, warm embrace. As I began to slide my hand slowly down her back to her waistband, I awoke. As I opened my eyes, I smiled and said to her, "That was wonderful! I hope we can do that again soon! I wouldn't mind waking up like that every morning."

Later, I was informed that because it didn't seem like a dream, because it seemed so real and was very brief and left me with such an incredibly joyful, peaceful feeling, it was actually not a dream, but it was a soul-joining. It was her soul's first interaction with me that I was aware of.

"Elusive Butterfly"

On Wednesday, as I was leaving to go somewhere (I don't recall where,) as I stood on the front step, I turned back to pull the front door shut, when a white butterfly fluttered right in front of me, close to my face and just staying there. A thought came into my mind as I watched it, transfixed, and I exclaimed, "I don't know if you're Mary Lee or not, but if you are, you're beautiful!" Then it immediately flew away.

I later shared with Joe about the butterfly, and he responded that very recently, he had also had a butterfly that lit on his shoulder, and he'd looked down at it and said, "Hi, Mom!" and it immediately flew away, too.

As time went on, I would see a white butterfly often, usually in the back yard. I felt it was somehow connected to her, and I was touched whenever I saw it. When I occasionally saw a second one dancing around with it, it always brought tears to my eyes, for I felt that it somehow represented both of us.

Sometime later, I learned that it was a universal belief all over the world, that white butterflies represent the souls of a loved one who had passed on.

I remember thinking that it was curious that I had been able to go to sleep each night and not awaken until the next morning. I seemed to have a peace that I didn't understand at the time, but nevertheless, I was grateful for it.

On Thursday, at the funeral home, we had calling during the afternoon and evening. My face had been operated on a few weeks earlier, and it hurt and felt swollen. Our family members told me it was red, and suggested I try to sit down more. In the evening, a couple from church, Marvin and Sally Teegardin, came over to me, and Sally quietly said something that I didn't hear, (my hearing after the accident was still not up to par) and Marvin sat down next to me and was talking to me and held my hand. I didn't understand what was happening. Among other things, he said, "I died, you know." I knew he'd had a stroke before I knew them, and I replied, "No, I didn't know that." Later, going home in the car, Joe said that Marvin had been channeling Mary Lee. I was upset and angry, and said, "It would have been nice if anyone had told *me*!" I was offended that they knew, but hadn't told me, or I would have understood what he (she) was saying to me. I felt robbed.

The next day, I called Sally, and she hadn't realized that I didn't hear what she'd quietly told us. She repeated to me most of what Mary Lee had said, including that she was checking on me to see if I was okay. Mary Lee's body was being cremated on that day.

Saturday afternoon, September 11, was her Memorial/Celebration Service at Unity Christ Church where we'd been very active members for over twenty-five years. I knew she would be there, and I thought to myself how amazed she must be to see the sanctuary packed with three hundred of her friends and relatives. She was always so unassuming, she had never realized how deeply loved and honored she was by so many, many people.

Michel Holland, a dear friend, opened the service with a sweet, touching solo, "To Where You Are." For many years, Mary Lee had sung in both of the choirs I directed, and a third choir joined with them to sing several songs during the service.

I wasn't aware of it yet, but Mary Lee had given me the right things to say and do for my part of her service, but I did know that she immediately helped me at one point when my voice shook slightly. She and I were able to set a light, sometimes joyful tone for the service by the gentle laughter some of my remarks and actions (and a few stuffed animals) had elicited.

When Jan and Joe came up, they were incredible! They elevated the mood of everyone even more. They were delightful and loving—and sweetly funny. Then a few dear friends shared their fond memories of her, the minister performed a releasing ceremony that I had requested, the combined choirs sang the benediction, and many people commented that it had indeed been a wonderful celebration of Mary Lee's life.

Two days after Mary Lee's Celebration Service, my younger sister, Jan Blain flew in from Nevada to be with me for a week that could have been very painful and lonely, with everyone leaving to go back home, back to their regular lives after the weekend. She wisely surmised that I would need her support even more then, than at the funeral home or during the funeral service.

Because I still wasn't well enough from the accident to drive much, she became my chauffeur for the week. Our first appointment was with Laurie Rainey Schmidt, a counselor and also a shaman, who had access to the spirit world when needed, had in the past sometimes counseled Mary Lee and me separately from time to time over the years, with an occasional session for us as a couple. Mostly, she reminded us of the strong, loving bond we shared, and of our need at times to remember to communicate verbally more fully with each other. I had also seen Laurie previously for some soul work, such as soul retrieval and healing on a soul level from a few traumatic experiences I had undergone.

Ever since the accident, and especially since Mary Lee's passing, I had felt frozen and stiff inside and was seeking healing from Laurie for my traumatized soul.

Mary Lee had fully trusted and appreciated Laurie's skill as a qualified counselor, but she also had a scientist's skepticism of the soul work that Laurie also practiced. I respected Mary Lee's judgment, but I had sometimes wished that she could find some soul-healing, as I had. I especially wished that kind of healing for her after the violent truck/car accident.

"Just My Imagination"

I invited Jan to stay in the room and watch the process, saying that I wanted her to see a part of my spiritual life that I had never shared with anyone in our family.

At the end of the process, Laurie told us that she had found that my soul had been literally frozen from the accident, and had to be shattered into pieces, which some other souls who had come to help, restored my soul to its wholeness once again.

Jan commented on how my face finally had a relaxed, peaceful appearance that she had not seen since she had arrived in town.

Then, Laurie told us about the soul journey itself. She said that she had been surprised to unexpectedly meet Mary Lee in the spirit world, standing there relaxed, with her arms crossed, and saying to her, "So this is what you do. Can I watch?"

Jan and I both burst out laughing. Jan said, "That sounds just like Mary Lee, always eager to learn." I said, "She sounds as if she's well and strong, with her sense of humor intact, and I obviously don't need to try to convince her anymore that there is a spirit world, because she's now a part of it!"

After I told Laurie of my earlier experience with the butterfly, she suggested that we both pay close attention to living things whose behavior seemed to be just a little bit off, because it was very likely that Mary Lee might have something to do with it; it was her way of interacting with us, and we needed to pay attention to it.

Later, as Jan and I sat quietly in the back yard, as Mary Lee and I had often enjoyed doing, we noticed a little goldfinch who was not feeding on the small thistle seed in its own feeder, but was sitting at the larger bird feeder, as if he (or she) was going to eat the much larger sunflower seeds. Once, Mary Lee and I had seen a goldfinch do this, but it quickly gave up and returned to its own feeder. This bird sat there for a long time and finally began bobbing its head up and down, as if it was actually eating the large seed and breaking it open with its tiny beak. We kept watching and quietly laughing at its antics, until I finally said to it, "I don't know if you're Mary Lee or not, but if you are, you're beautiful . . . but you're also really strange!" Then, it immediately flew back to its own feeder and proceeded to actually eat.

We continued watching and enjoying the yard, when Jan said to me, "There's a bunny over by the side of the shed." It was on the far side of the yard.

My face was still somewhat swollen from the facial reconstructive surgery I'd undergone just nine days after the accident, so I couldn't wear glasses yet and wasn't able to see distant things very clearly. I replied, "Where? I can't see it." Immediately the bunny moved a little bit forward from under the bush. I quietly said, "I saw something move just now, but I can't see what it is." It moved a couple of feet farther out, and I said, "Now I can kind of see it, but not very clearly." Then it moved sideways, so its little brown body was right in front of the yellow wall of the shed, where I could see it much better. And he (or she) just sat there peacefully for a long time, while we quietly sat there, watching it in amazement!

Several months later, when I had an opportunity to ask Mary Lee if her soul had actually been in the butterfly, the bird, or the bunny during these experiences, she answered, "No, but my soul had an agreement with each of their souls." If I had ever wondered whether animals had souls, the answer was immediately settled firmly in my mind from her response to me.

original painting by Jan Blain, Pat's sister

SOME RESPONSES FROM LOVED ONES:

An early reply to my e-mail to loved ones, sent soon after the night of my releasing Mary Lee, was from Teresa Bucher, a Unity friend of deep spiritual insight and wisdom. I wept as I read it, but I soon realized that it was the beginning of the healing of my grief:

Thank you, Pat. You gave Mary Lee great gifts on this day. You gave her permission to leave if that is what she/her soul desired. Thank You!

This is often difficult for so many people, but you and she have an understanding of Soul and Loving that many don't yet know.

You gave her the gift of assurance and you affirmed your on-going love for one another. I know you will miss her touch, her voice, her smell, her laughter . . . her very presence.

On this night/early morning, you touched her and you spoke with her as if she would answer. Please know that in this experience, some people are so uncomfortable they are not able to be with one another in very important and intimate ways. You did everything . . . YOU did Everything you could, and you gave Mary Lee exquisite gifts.

You gave . . . thinking only about what is best for Mary Lee and her soul's journey. You gave without thought of anything in return. I think this is what St. Francis meant when he said, "Let me be an instrument of Your Love."

I hope you know that Mary Lee had the freedom to continue her journey because she knows your character, your strengths, your inner gifts, your capacity for Loving, and the qualities of your Soul. She knows you have the power to endure and that you will find a way to live, honoring all that she gave—you will live fully.

I know that with her absence, your life has changed forever. With her death, something precious has gone out of your life. I also know that without Mary Lee, you would not be who you are.

She has touched so many people, and they too, would not be the same, had they not encountered this extraordinary woman.

There is a Hebrew proverb that reads: There is a time to mourn, and now is your time. Blessed are those who mourn . . . you will be comforted.

Please know that you (we) mourn and you (we) grieve Mary Lee's death—because you (we) love her. Mary Lee will be missed. She will be missed because she is loved.

And others . . .

. . . I know that women like you and Mary Lee paved the way for us to be able to live openly and create our family. I am grateful to have met you and seen you both together as a loving couple. She was a gem, as are you." Laura

. . . the memorial service was an amazing tribute to an amazing woman. She was so important to the world and women's movement; I loved the stories about marching! . . . you and others did all the work; I thank you for that! You were so brave at the service; what you shared was a true inspiration to me about what life, love and relationship really mean. I miss seeing you and Mary Lee sitting together at church; we could just see the love and FUN in your faces. You always had your arm around her.

Pat, you continue to inspire as we see you moving through pain and grief with a loving smile for others on your face. Mary Lee would be so proud! Love, Mary B.

And from Betty H., who had previously lost her beloved husband, Flave,

I was so touched when I read your tribute to Mary Lee. Flave and I had such a deep love for each other, and I always felt that you and Mary Lee had that same deep love ... Flave will always be with me, just as Mary Lee will be with you; what sweet and loving memories we are blessed with.

Dear Aunt Pat,

Just wanted to let you know you are in my thoughts, and I hope you are resuming normal activities and finding peace and solace. I enjoyed learning [from her obituary] about what an extraordinary person Mary Lee was. I was also pleased [the night of the calling at the funeral home] that you sat next to me at dinner, and that we were able able to talk at some length. I really enjoyed that.

Take care. Love, Geoff

At times like this words are inadequate—but memories are not. We will miss Mary Lee. Bud and Peggy

Some friends from the Xena Conventions:

Dearest Pat, Our love and prayers are with you, and we keep you in our hearts daily. We wish you peace in your soul ... please know that we are out here for you. You both touched our lives and we have such fond memories of our gatherings. We hope our friendship will live on in you ... All our love, Rhys and Erika

We are so sorry about Mary Lee. Your love was such an inspiration ... Knowing the both of you has touched our lives. Love, Sarah V. and Lynn B.

Pat, Thinking of you. Take your time, go at your own pace. Do what you need to do. Grief is bitter and sweet. It is individual. No one can tell you how to get through it. Always remember that you are surrounded by those of us who love you and support you. Nancy C

Pat, We are holding you in our hearts and sending you loving energy.

I have to tell you that we are paying a tribute to Mary Lee nearly every day. I have never been one to wear a seatbelt unless Nita nags me enough. Now whenever we get in the car, alone or together, we have the "Mary Lee Rule"—We don't move until everyone is buckled up. I'm ashamed to say it took such a horrible loss for me to wise up. She continues to teach, doesn't she? [I wept as I read this]

We appreciated the information and photo you sent with Mary Lee's lovely Christmas card.

All our best, Cat & Nita

From some of my early journal entries in September 2010: I'm still doing, doing, doing every day and night, to push away the grief . . . and there's so very much to do. Many strange dreams, some are about animals' deaths . . . and coming back to life.

In October, I began choir rehearsals a month later than usual. Later, I wrote that I needed to stop the driven work, driven extra eating, reluctance to sit down or lie down, and to stop using "doing" to stave off loneliness and grief.

October 6—A beautiful, lavender Rose of Sharon plant has suddenly grown tall and blossomed just outside the kitchen window. We never planted it; the birds dropped the seeds. I thanked Mary Lee for sending me this unusual encouragement. In December, I had it transplanted over in front of the bedroom bay window. The gardener who had come said it was highly unusual for this kind of plant to blossom this late in the year. When I said I believed Mary Lee had caused it to spring up to comfort me, he said he absolutely believed that loving spirits do that sort of thing; he'd seen it in his own life. Often, when I sometimes share a bit about Mary Lee's activities, the other person immediately shares similar kinds of activities with a loved one (mother, grandfather, etc.) who had passed on.

When I try to meditate, sometimes all I can do is cry and express my loneliness.

A lot had been happening in December. I wrote of some things I learned since her passing.

I realized her soul's joy at being freed from her aging and injured body.

I learned that when we in Unity pray for a peaceful transition for a loved one who is crossing over, it isn't instantaneous, and that she's gradually learning more and more on the other side, just as I'm learning on this side how to recognize and respond to her when she's in touch with me.

I expressed gratitude for Sally and Marvin T., Carolyn C., Devonee L/H. and Teresa B., all of whom had been my teachers about so many matters of the spirit that I had been learning, and many more that I had yet to learn, about what my Murdy's spiritual journey is like, and how much longer it will take than I'd ever imagined.

I thanked Steven M. for counseling me when I was desolate and afraid and feeling incredibly lonely. He recommended that I read the book *Life After Life*, written in 1975 by Dr. Raymond Moody. Any readers who have lost a person dear to you should read this book. It's probably in your public library.It can help you to know that what we call death is so much more involved and hopeful, beautiful, and joyful than we ever dreamed.

I am grateful to learn that Mary Lee's soul and mine are indeed, still very connected, and that we're each continuing our life-long learning adventure . . . even as we are (for right now) on different sides of this human earth school and the spirit world.

I learned from Teresa that some Native American tribes had a sacred tradition of giving away belongings of the deceased, as a way of honoring him or her. There was a high value placed on giving away and sharing what is ours. Also, it was said that this giving brings about healing for those mourning their loss.

So, one Saturday, the night of our choir party, I filled many tables with Mary Lee's belongings, explained the Indian custom to the choir members, and invited them to take anything they wanted, as a remembrance of her; she was much loved. I know that for me, it was healing on that very evening, as some of her dear friends proudly showed me what they had taken to remember her by.

The next day, after the church service, I invited all of the congregation to go down to the fellowship hall, look over the many things that had belonged to Mary Lee (and sometimes both of us) and take as many of those things as they liked, so they would have something of hers, to honor and remember her. I urged them to take as much as they wanted, and to be extremely generous with themselves. I remarked that I would be incredibly pleased and thankful if those tables were virtually empty of anything, so I wouldn't have to take anything back home. It not only brought me healing, but also a gradual sense of order in our home, by disseminating much of what would have become a great deal of clutter to me.

Also, I knew Mary Lee's soul would be pleased to know that her friends now have a small part of her, too. I also was sure that she was present and had watched all this happening.

> *"Lean on Me"*

When I'm distraught and mournful, grieving her physical loss and I ask her to help me, a mantle of comforting peace gently descends over me; it's truly a peace that passes understanding!

> *"I Wanna Hold Your Hand"*

Once, I told her how much I missed not being able to hold hands with her—we'd always done that a lot, mostly in private. As I lay on top of our bedcover, I felt a warmth come into the back of my hands that I had never felt before. Somewhat amazed, I asked if she was holding my hands, and the warmth became slightly more pronounced. She still continues to do that from time to time. Some days later, I was aware of that same warmth in my hands, and then I also felt it on my lips. I asked, "Are you kissing me on my mouth?!" Her response was a lot of fast kisses, as if she was excited to know that I'd figured out what she was doing. I laughed with happiness.

She makes me laugh in surprise and joy when she obviously moves things from their regular place, such as a small sign I keep on top of the left speaker in the Rainbow Room. I work on choir things with my back to the speakers, sometimes creating a CD for several hours, and when I go over to turn that speaker off, the sign has been turned as much as 180 degrees—nothing subtle about it. That's another way she shows her support and appreciation for the work I've been doing in that room. Sometimes she moves the stuffed frog several inches back from the two little bear angels I keep on the ledge of the china cabinet in the kitchen; I always keep the frog's chin on top of the cloud that the little kissing/giggling bears sit on, so he's always very close to them.

She shows her encouragement for what I'm doing by causing the doorbell extension (plugged into an electrical outlet in the Rainbow Room) to ring—and sometimes stutter or sound slower and with a lower pitch without having it ring in the living room, where it would ordinarily originate.

Once, when I was having all the carpets in the house deep cleaned, she rang the door chimes haphazardly and over and over, sounding like they were either very drunk or very excited. I figured it was the latter, and chuckled.

Especially when I ask, she helps me to find lost things, by leading me to look in the right place by accident. I go into the room for something else, and suddenly notice what I'd been looking for—sometimes on the floor or on top of a cabinet.

After a while, I began to realize that when I would listen to the car radio, she gave me songs that expressed her love for me and her promise that her love (and she) will be with me forever. Even now, she sometimes gives me one song after another, and they're always right on the spot for something that just happened to me or for something I've been thinking or feeling at that moment. Sometimes I'm moved to tears, sometimes I laugh, sometimes I sing along, but it's always clear that she's talking to me. The music (and she) moves me and makes me feel so incredibly lucky to have such an amazing, thoughtful and loving soulmate so closely in touch with me.

Toward the end of this book, I've compiled an extensive (alphabetical) list of the titles of songs she's given me, beginning sometime in 2011. I finally stopped writing them down in May, 2014. Now, I just enjoy them, and thank her for them, and sometimes just sing along.

Often as soon as I awaken in the morning, before I am even thinking about the day, she gives me ideas and inspiration about solving problems or about activities for me to initiate that day, or longer projects for me to undertake, or someone to contact that I hadn't thought about. She refers to this as whispering in my ear.

She's my great incentive to learn to live my life in tune with all things of the spirit, to grow spiritually, so I'll be more sensitive to and aware of her spirit, as well as my own.

If you can, search out the lyrics of the songs,

> *"Elusive Butterfly"*
> *"Pure Imagination"*

"Elusive Butterfly" and "Pure Imagination," about learning to notice and pay attention to, trust my imagination and intuition, to begin to learn to see and hear her, but without using my five human senses.

The only thing that remained of Mary Lee's car after the accident was a license plate, which years before, I had purchased for her in Shipshewana at one of the many tables of interesting items at the large flea market there. It had a hummingbird, and the message I had them paint on it was "Love nature." I asked the car insurance agent to send it to me, and now it's on the front of my car. Every time I look at it, I think of her, and many people comment on the beauty and uniqueness of it.

I now look at butterflies, birds, and bunnies as sweet souls and new friends, and I sometimes talk to them, expressing my love and appreciation for them whenever I see them in our back yard . . . or anywhere else. Each of the things I've written about here, whenever they occur, I talk to Mary Lee and thank her for making me more aware of her presence, and I also tell her that I love her.

She knows what I'm thinking and what I'm feeling. She's present with me most of the time, but she doesn't always interact with me.

I visualize her now, on the other side, as being stronger, wiser, and much more knowledgeable and aware than I am right now. That's why I want to keep learning from her, and I want to continue to grow spiritually throughout the rest of my life.

She's helping me to learn to get to know my own soul better.

I'm learning more and more to trust my intuition and inspiration, and to act on it.

She helps me to have courage and wisdom, to live a life of joy.

She often makes me laugh, and she always makes me know that I am loved and cherished.

We often used to tell each other, "You're God's greatest gift to me!" And she still is.

Here are a couple of the songs she's given me that express what's in my heart as I write this chapter:

"You Light Up My Life"
She continues to encourage me to carry on . . .

"When I Need You"
I close my eyes . . . and she's here with me . . .

Thank you, Sweet Woman!

Chapter 9
Shocking and Amazing Information!

Read this if you dare!

> *"Oh, Ho, Ho, It's Magic"*
> *"Have to Believe We Are Magic"*
> *"Pure Imagination"*
> *"I Believe in Angels"*

Three months after Mary Lee's passing, I finally worked up the courage to have my first meeting with Tina Zion, a fourth-generation psychic, intuitive teacher, holistic healer, and counselor with afterlife experiences, who had been highly recommended to me by Laurie Rainey Schmidt, and who would finally be able to put me in direct contact with my dear Mary Lee.

I never, never, *never* thought I'd ever be doing anything like this!

The following contains some of the things I've learned since Dec. 6, 2010, when Jannie, Mary Lee's daughter, and I were at my first meeting with Tina.

When we first met Tina, Mary Lee's first comment to us was, "Well, finally!" She had been waiting and waiting for me to work up the courage to take this important step toward actually being able to hear from her and to converse with her.

When Jannie asked her mom how long she would be active in our lives as she had been since her death, Mary Lee promised to be active in our lives until it's our time. In other words, for the rest of our lives! I didn't expect that, but it gave me great relief. When my time comes, Mary Lee told me that she will be front and center, to welcome me, and will hold my hand through my journey.

I asked her if my releasing her at Parkview Hospital on Sunday, September 5, 2010, to go on with her soul journey had been helpful to her; she responded that yes, she had been fighting the process and was trying to stay here for my sake, and that it had made "all the difference in the world . . . all the difference in the world!"

She also told me, "You need to lose the heaviness about the accident." I'd sometimes felt sadness and guilt from my responsibility for our even being there and the timing of it, and I often had feelings of regret and "if only . . ." She said, "You didn't bring it about, but *we* had already chosen the way it would end, even before we were born, while we were still in the spirit world together." She explained, "We had several options of how to end it, and this was the one that we *both* chose, because it would bring about the most spiritual growth in Pat afterwards." Her words were as if she had turned off a switch inside me, immediately removing my torment, because of this new information that it was *our pre-chosen plan.*

She tells me that she has a much broader perspective and sees a bigger picture, now that she's in the spirit world, and that she now has memories and much information that she didn't have while still in her human body.

"A Woman in Love"

Her personality, intelligence, wit, sense of humor, love and devotion and compassion are all still very much intact, as they were when she was in her body.

She is still the unassuming, somewhat private being that she was during our shared lifetime, and she was sometimes reticent to speak to me as a soul-mate/lover in front of Tina. At first, she even spoke of Tina as "We don't need this woman!" But I did!

Sometime later, I invited my younger sister Jan to come with me to a session with Tina, and I believe it was life changing for her. Mary Lee sat between Jan and me, and at one point, my Murdy turned to Jan and asked, "Do you realize what a sweet soul you are?" Jan and I both had tears at that, as I answered, "No, I don't think she does." She had more conversation with Jan during the session; Tina had made a recording of the whole hour and gave both Jan and me a CD of the recording. When she went home to Nevada, she and John, her husband, listened to it together. I believe it changed both of their lives!

In response to my curiosity about just how she rings the doorbell in the Rainbow Room without having it ring at the front door, she giggled as she described exactly what she does to set it off. It *is* funny; she said she sticks her fingers into the socket and wiggles them around until the chimes ring! Tina and I both laughed at that. When I asked her if sometime I could actually watch her move something, she demurred. I still haven't been able to watch it happen, so it always surprises me and makes me laugh.

I was recently looking over some of the journaling I was doing for the first three or four months after her passing, and I realize now that she was trying to interact with me by varying what she was doing (I guess she didn't want me to get bored by using same-old-same-old) but it only caused me confusion, uncertainty, and anxiety.

In early January, I complained to her that she seemed to be interacting more often with Danny (Jannie's husband) in obvious ways, so they would recognize that it was her, and I was feeling neglected; Mary Lee replied that she didn't want to clunk and thump things with me, because I was her soulmate, and she wanted to do it in a more personal way for me.

At home one evening I tearfully told her that lately she didn't seem to be as loving or caring. I felt like she didn't love me enough to do anything to relieve my distress and pleading and crying. I finally said angrily, "I give up! I can't do this anymore! You never do anything obvious for me, and when I do finally figure out that it's something that you're doing, you don't do that anymore. It's like you're playing games with me, and I can't take it anymore—I I'm done with this—I *quit!*"

In effect, I was breaking up with her, and it was devastating. Grieving, I went into the bathroom to get ready for bed, feeling depressed and beaten down. I put the toothpaste on my toothbrush and as I began to brush my teeth, I glanced at the small three-tiered triangular shelf on the wall to my left, and did a pronounced double-take at what I saw on the bottom two shelves. I always kept my black comb lying on the bottom shelf with my box of powder, and her comb was always lying on the middle shelf. But now, both of those combs were standing *upright*, with their *tines* pointing *up!* My powder box was backwards, with the lid up, bracing my comb in place. I was astonished and relieved, and I burst into tears, thanking her and saying, "Now, *that's* obvious!! And funny! Thank you, Sweetheart!" And I never gave up on her again.

At the end of one of the first sessions with Tina, Mary Lee remarked that "we're both learning to do it better." That is, to communicate with each other better.

During one session, Tina told me that as I spoke, Mary Lee was standing next to me and had just said, "Even now, we both continue to be much stronger when we're together," and also that she likes being with me. Mary Lee has stressed that she's not trapped here in this world, but rather that she chooses to be here. She says that she is also learning from my progress on this side, and that it makes her spirit lighter; she says that we're continuing to learn from each other, just as we did when we were both on this side.

Tina once mentioned that lately, Mary Lee's appearance seems to be getting slightly younger than before.

She sometimes comes and goes during a session. Once, I later found that she had not even come in at all, during two or three intensely personal counseling sessions I'd had with Tina—she later told me that she hadn't wanted to infringe on my privacy. I was surprised, but also touched and relieved to hear her say this.

In a later session, I told her of donating some of her clothes to places for women in need that we had both supported, like Charis House, for homeless women and children, the Women's Shelter, and that I had taken her more professional clothing to Women in Transition, where a woman could wear them to a job interview and present a more professional image. I had even taken her lab coats and other scientific supplies and items to Darlene Bender at the IPFW Biology Department. Mary Lee said she approved and was very pleased.

She was also pleased when I told her of giving many of her things to friends and choir members and both her family and my family, who all had dearly loved her. Mary Lee responded, "You have given all of those things wings and have made my spirit lighter!" Tina suddenly laughed, and said she was seeing lots of little things with tiny little wings, flying around in the air. She also said that Mary Lee's spirit had floated up higher than it had been before.

One morning I awoke and went into the living room to find a haphazard pile of papers in front of the printer, on the floor. They were about fifteen to twenty pages from a sample of this book (titled "Teeny Weeny Teaser") with a blank page where pages forty-five and forty-six should haven been. I was mystified, and the possibility of an impish Mary Lee being involved briefly crossed my mind. The next day, I asked Mary Lee about it, and she giggled like a little kid and said she started to do it, " . . . but something went haywire." Tina and I laughed and told her that it ended up on the floor because I had folded the paper tray back when I logged off and went to bed that night. What a hoot! I still laugh every time I picture what happened. Ironically those two blank pages told of when her body died and when she began to interact with me soon after; I think maybe she didn't want to print those?

I had a dream about Dad, and when I awoke, I told him I loved him and that I hope he's okay. I wished him a happy life, full of love.

Sometime early in 2010, Mary Lee had asked me what I would do if she had to go into into a nursing home. I believe she was thinking about her getting older and fearing that we'd have to live apart. I remember replying that I'd take care of her in our home, with the aid of home health care. I thought carefully about it and told her that if she had to go into a nursing home, I'd come and be with her there. Remembering this conversation months after her death, I wept when I realized that I hadn't been able to keep those promises. When she was at the Rehabilitation Hospital after the accident and her traumatic brain injury, she would call me, over and over, begging me to bring her home, begging me to stay with her. I'm crying now, as I recall how I couldn't do either, partially because of my own injuries and their rules there. I'm so, so sorry, my Love.

I wept again as I re-read that passage, and as I type it here.

As I enter our darkened bedroom, Mary Lee flashes the lamp by the bed as I reach out for it, but just before I touch it. Once, after a subtle flash, I said, "I love you!" And she immediately flashed again in response.

When Mary Lee had been still alive on this side, I'd had a fairly strong belief in reincarnation, but she always made it clear that she didn't believe in it. During one session, I asked her if we had ever been together in previous lifetimes, and she immediately responded that "we've been together for twenty-seven different lifetimes, over a period of more than one thousand years! Though not always as lovers." In a later session, I asked Mary Lee more specifically how many years did our twenty-seven lives cover, and she answered, "One thousand and nineteen." Note: She had already been repeatedly sending me the song, "I've Loved You for a Thousand Years."

She also volunteered that "this is the first of those lives that Pat hasn't been a man!" She explained that my soul had wanted to learn more about the emotional aspect of a woman during this lifetime, by being born female this time. I was amazed to hear of this. Mary Lee then said she has always been a woman in each of our lives together, and she mused lightly, "Maybe sometime I'll come back as a man." I answered, "Or maybe not."

When I expressed curiosity about how long I have yet to live in this body, this life, she said that she wasn't supposed to tell me, and because of that, she hasn't been given that information.

During one session, she did something that we often used to do to each other—Tina told me that her spirit, standing next to me, had just leaned down and kissed me on the top of my head. This brought me to tears, and still does, when I remember it. I told Tina that often, when one of us used to pass by the other one who was seated at the kitchen table, the one walking by would bend down and plant a kiss on the crown of the other. Ever since that session, Tina now informs me when Mary Lee kisses me on top of my head.

Since her physical death, she has helped me to write several things by inspiring me with thoughts that just pour out effortlessly—including much of this book. That's why I like to refer to Mary Lee as my very own ghost writer!

Sometime in 2011, Tina had suggested that I be on the lookout for signs that might be sent from Mary Lee. During my drive to and from Tina's office, Mary Lee had begun to speak to me through many of the songs on the radio. When I first told Tina about this, she enthusiastically said, "That's huge! It's a logical way for her to communicate with you, through music."

A question I've asked her more recently: On April 6, I said that for the first time in public, Larry Heral will be singing the song he recently composed for us, a tribute to our relationship—I said to her, "I'm inviting you to attend the concert; will you sit with me? I'll save a chair for you, and I'll tell anyone who tries to sit in it that this chair is reserved for you." Her response was, "Maybe you could make a sign with my name on it, to put on the chair." I enthusiastically told her that I would. And I did. And I felt her presence that night. The song got a long, enthusiastic ovation from the large crowd. And even though people in the audience often looked for a seat during the concert, no one asked to use her chair. That sign was a great idea.

I once said to Mary Lee, "In the Rainbow Room, you often move the little sign that's on top of the left speaker while I work on choir stuff with my back to it, and then when I'm finished and I turn around, I see how you've moved that sign in various ways. The last time, did you toss it on the floor?" She laughed and said yes, she had. She's always did have a healthy, fun-loving kid inside her, and I still love her continued playfulness!

Once, I invited my mom, (Lois) to a session with Tina and Mary Lee. I had always pulled up a chair for Mary Lee to sit in, and as we talked, Tina looked past us and said, "There's a white-haired woman standing there on the other side of the room." I exclaimed, "That's my mom!" and immediately began to pull up another chair. Tina remarked that she hadn't asked for a chair, and I replied, "She wouldn't have asked; she wouldn't want to be a bother." Later in that same session, Tina remarked, "Your mom and Mary Lee are sitting there holding hands." I told her I thought it was touching and wonderful, that they evidently were good friends in the spirit world. I was especially glad for Mom, since I knew that her life here had often not been happy or rewarding for her.

In the summer of 2013, we were planning to bring together the largest family reunion we've ever had, with forty-seven out of a possible fifty-three of us attending. During my last session with Tina before leaving for the reunion in Elko, Nevada, Mary Lee firmly told me, "This will be a wonderful high point of your life!"

As I awoke from a nap in my room at the Elko hotel before the festivities began, I actually saw Mom at the foot of my bed, and I recognized her! I told her I was surprised to see her, but suddenly realized that of course she would be here—it was a reunion of people she and Dad were responsible for bringing into the world! I told her how happy I was to see her and had a new awareness of her presence. Later that evening, I made a speech to them all, telling them how proud I was of our family, how I loved our diversity and the goodness of each of us, from the youngest to the oldest. I spoke of how Mom and Dad were good, honest, and hard-working people who did the best they could in life, and through their example all five of us siblings had learned and lived those qualities as we grew up and eventually passed them on to the next generation(s).

After returning home, I again invited both Mary Lee and Mom to my next session with Tina, where they both informed me that while I spoke into that microphone about our family, they had both been up there with me, standing on either side of me. I was stunned, but very pleased. Tina smiled, sharing that what they had just told us had given her good chills, and I felt incredibly blessed and supported by both of them! I think they both had a great time at the reunion.

Recently, I've been blessed with the addition of two new members of my healing team who are both very spiritually aware. First was Dyanne Gregg who gave me Reiki (healing energy) treatments and later worked with Mary Lee during each session. As Mary Lee and Dyanne have gotten to know each other better, Mary Lee has taken part in the sessions, giving advice about specific places where I need the healing, protecting me from any pain, and even taking part in doing some Reiki herself, usually on my left shoulder. The first time I felt Dyanne's touch move to my right leg but I *still* felt the touch on my left shoulder, and even felt it shift slightly, I was amazed, and joked that I thought that Mary Lee was learning Reiki from Dyanne! This continued to happen since that first time. Recently, at the end of the session, Dyanne shared with me that they had recently had to put down their beloved dog, and she had worried about it, wondering if they had done the right thing. She told me that during that session, Mary Lee had held that dog in her arms, showing it to Dyanne, to assure her that it had been the right decision, and that her dog was fine, healthy, and happy. Dyanne shared with me that she had wept tears of relief and healing from that thoughtful act of Mary Lee. I told her that Mary Lee was not only a loving soul, but also a kind one. She agreed, and said it was a blessing for her to know both Mary Lee and me.

Several months after my back surgery I met Angie Netterville, who has begun a Hands On revolutionary kind of physical therapy with me, and who can also see Mary Lee's aura and can feel her touch and presence. She is very spiritually aware, and continues to learn to develop that aspect of her life and to use it in her treatments, sometimes with the help of the workshops and classes that Tina often offers. As a matter of fact, at one of these workshops, Angie and Dyanne met for the first time, and they both felt an immediate, strong connection, as if they'd found a long-lost friend. I told them each that their souls were probably good friends in the spirit world, even though their human minds had no memory of it. See, I'm learning, too.

As Mary Lee gets better acquainted with both Dyanne and Angie, she has been more playful with them. I think she's enjoying helping with my healing.

Tina has recently told me that Mary Lee's energy is stronger than it used to be since she crossed over, and that she's more light-hearted lately. I've noticed that some of the surprising things she does and the songs she continues to give me often make me laugh as I thank her for them.

Toward the end of May, 2014, during a Reiki session with Dyanne, she told me that besides both of us and Mary Lee, there was someone else present: an older woman, who seemed to be a special friend of Mary Lee. I asked if she was short and had white hair, and she said, "Yes." I told her, "That's my mom!" Dyanne told me that when she had placed one of her hands on my upper abdomen, they both came over and each added her hand on top of hers. Shortly after, (I don't know why,) I took my hand out from under the light blanket, and she told me that I had put my hand on top of both of theirs! She asked me if I had felt them, and I replied that I hadn't been aware of what was happening, and that when I put my hand on my abdomen, I was surprised that Dyanne's fingers were there, but I had no idea that there were also two other hands in the"stack!

Mary Lee also displayed to Dyanne the healing embrace ring, to show her that she approved of my recent gift of those matching rings of ours to both her and Angie. I'm pretty sure she had whispered in my ear to give me the idea of doing that; I had told each of them that the rings were from both of us. Then, Mom began to show Dyanne early photos of two young boys, one with darker hair, and I told her they were my older brothers, when they were young! Mom kept showing Dyanne more pictures from our past, which I identified, as she described them. I told her how proud Mom was of all of us, but that she often didn't tell us directly. I was surprised, but very pleased that Mom had now shown up at one of my healing sessions without my having given her a special invitation to come. I think she knows now how much I welcome her presence. Later, after I arrived home, I spoke to Mom, telling her that I'm realizing now that there are not just two, but three of us sharing this home. That pleases me a great deal.

I had mentioned to Dyanne that I had actually seen (and recognized) Mom just once, at the Deihl Reunion in 2013, but although I'd been asking Mary Lee to show herself to me, she never has. I said I was pretty sure she never would, until it was my time, and she had come to welcome me and to lead me to my next place of existence. Earlier, Tina had wondered if it might be too upsetting for me; Dyanne wondered if maybe I wouldn't want to let her go. I don't think either idea would be true, but I told Dyanne that if I actually were able to actually see her with my own eyes, I just might ask her to do it again . . . and again . . . and again . . . and . . . I haven't ever heard her voice, either.

Today (July, 2014) Angie told me how much she's been learning from both Mary Lee and me, and what a privilege it is to get to know us better. Wow!

In one session, I asked Mary Lee if this was the first time she'd been this involved in interacting with the survivor of us, and if she'd ever before been so active as she had in my life. She responded that whoever died first did interact with the other one. Sometimes it was her, and sometimes it was me. I was surprised at her response.

Sometimes Tina calls to my attention a new, more profound awareness I am gradually developing over time. I told her of a dream I'd had that Mary Lee and I had both just died, and we were talking to someone who could see and hear us, telling them about how some things we now knew made sense, and things fit into place for us. They could see and hear us, and didn't know we had died.

I had told Judith, my gardner, about how Mary Lee had whispered in my ear to give her the little gardening angel statue to her, and how she follows her around as she works, and sometimes whispering in her ear about things for her to do. Judith had thanked me for telling her of this and said that she often had the feeling that someone was watching her; she would sometimes look up at a window, to see if someone

there was watching her. Judith is another person who has entered my life who is also very spiritually aware.

These past four and a half years have been an altogether remarkable spiritual journey for me!

Wonderful people have been coming into my life who are loving, authentic, centered, and spiritually aware, healing and joy-filled friends and professionals. I love and admire them all.

What I do and what I dream include thee...

My Mary Lee,
I will love you
always and forever.
Your Pat

And I continue to learn from them all

and enjoy the journey

which is called

L I F E !

To contact Tina, use the phone number listed on her business card. She does many phone sessions with people all over the world; no need to be in the room with her.

Chapter 10
Our Life Together Progresses . . . And Continues On

> *"Up Where We Belong"*

In 2011, I had decided that I wouldn't be doing any travelling, because that was something Mary Lee and I had always enjoyed doing together, and it would be too lonely for me to travel alone.

Then, one morning I awoke with the sudden thought that I could fly to Nevada to visit with about twenty members of my family who are living there. My sister Jan was planning to drive to Elko in July, with her husband John and their beloved little dog, Maggie, and all of us could spend some time together.

I mentioned this idea in my next session with Tina, and Mary Lee immediately said, "I've been thinking about making a journey." Suddenly, I realized that I wouldn't be alone on the plane or during the visit. Mary Lee advised me to simply be aware of and pay attention to her presence there.

I called Jan, we made hotel arrangements, and I asked her if she could coordinate a time schedule to accommodate each of the many family members there, so that I could meet with them in small groups, and get to know each of them better, especially the young people, asking each one about their hopes, dreams, and plans for their future. I also wanted to tell them about the soft spoken but also highly accomplished woman they had seen about every four years thoughout their childhood, from the time they were babies. I realized later that my plans for that trip developed gradually, as my Mary Lee kept whispering in my ear with more good ideas of what I wanted to do.

Jan went with me to each appointment, quietly listening as I talked with each one, and (as she later shared with me,) being amazed at what I said and did, to demonstrate my generous support and encouragement of each of their dreams for the future.

I had a wonderful time talking with each of them, helping them to know both Mary Lee and me better as individuals and not just as Aunt Pat and her friend, and I was learning more about them as individuals, watching their amazement and joy, as I surprised each with an unexpected gift. It gave me great joy with each of these interactions, and I suddenly realized I was finding a new joy in my life without Mary Lee, as several of my dear friends had advised me to do, in the loving sympathy cards they had sent to me less than a year earlier.

When I returned home, I continued this new way of living, getting to know some friends better, not by just making small talk, but by learning more about them and their lives, and if possible, by lightening their burden in any way I could. Their joy-filled surprise continues to fill me with this new joy; also, it has become a part of my new way of living my life.

I've also come to believe that we can become more open to our Highest Good and that we can co-create an incredibly fulfilling life by our positive, uplifting thoughts, attitudes and actions about ourselves, others, events and situations in our lives. My strong and still growing belief in Divine Order has continued to change my life and me . . . for the better.

In December 2011, I was visiting Jan and John Blain and celebrating Christmas with them and my brother Bob in Nevada, and John privately asked me how to interact with Jan after he dies. I replied, "You'll know when and how to. Your soul will see the bigger picture, and you'll have knowledge you didn't have when your body was alive."

During that same visit, Jan and I were preparing to record a four-hand accompaniment of "Love Is a Song" on her new piano. The first recording was just okay, so I asked Mary Lee to help us do it, but the second recording wasn't as good. We deleted that one and stopped, so I could ask my Murdy to help us all to focus, so we could do it even better. John was removing the first half of the music for us each time. That time was very good, and we all thanked Mary Lee for her help! Earlier, we weren't confident that we could do it.

Then when Jan and I came into the living room, she was going to say something to John, but she couldn't. She froze, and said, "My whole body is suddenly tingling!" Afterwards, I told her I had an idea that it was Mary Lee contacting her. She agreed and was amazed by that brief experience. She seemed awed by it.

Later, John said, "I want Mary Lee to ring our doorbell." He wants her to interact with him, just as she'd been doing that day with my left hearing aid and in other ways. I replied, "I never know what she's going to do or when, but you might learn to pay attention to anything that seemed a little off or unusual." I later found that she had tried to push their doorbell, but for some reason couldn't do it. She told me to have them pay attention to the lamp between their chairs,

that she would be turning that on. Some weeks later, she did it, but since it was during the day, they weren't aware of it. So she turned on the ceiling fan—on the fastest speed, which they never used, and Jan walked into the room and said, "John, did you turn on the fan?" He replied, "No." They both realized Mary Lee had done it, and they were so thrilled and happy, they called me to tell me about it!

Jan and John have both been growing and progressing spiritually, because they've both been open to and accepting of my incredible experiences with Mary Lee. Also, they have been reading together the very positive and inspirational Daily Word every morning. Jan shared with me that it was very different from other devotional books she'd read, and she and John really like the way it begins each day for them.

My brother Bob has also gone through some remarkable changes during the first two years that he also began living in Mesquite, Nevada. He often had a more positive outlook, he was more relaxed and happier, and he smiled and laughed more. I think this part of his life could be much more rewarding and joyful, and I'm so pleased for him.

My first morning back home, I awoke very happily with a peaceful joy, and I felt Mary Lee's energy in me as I pulled open the bedroom drapes, expressing gratitude for the beautiful yard and our wonderful home, when a bunny suddenly appeared from behind the shed. I hadn't seen any since late last summer. I laughed and said I was glad to see him, and I loved him and thanked him for the welcome back home greeting. I also thanked Mary Lee for arranging it for me.

Soon, I spent another enjoyable Christmas celebration with my sister Margie and Larry and their family, daughter Roxanne and Jeff and their children: Samantha and Nathan and also their son Jonathon and Martha, with their three boys: Devin, Lucas, and baby Ryan. After things had settled down, and Margie and I were alone, she shared with me that she and

Larry were beginning to be curious about the spirit world, ever since she had read the book I'd loaned her, titled *Life After Life*. She had sought out other books that had more information about things of the spirit.

Once, I was unplugging an extension cord that was behind Mary Lee's dresser in her bedroom, when I knocked a small framed photo of us off the wall and onto the floor behind the dresser. There was no way I could move the dresser. I brought in several tools and a flashlight so I could see it, and I put a picker-upper tool down but couldn't see what I was doing. I said to Mary Lee, "I'm gonna need some help!" Trusting that it would work as I blindly used the tool and began to bring it up, I was delighted to see the picture when I lifted it up far enough to be able to see it! I thanked her so much, and I also learned to:

Ask for help
Trust in that help
Take action, in faith
Give thanks!

My January 13 journal entry: "I had a very sweet dream last night; Mary Lee and I were in bed, and she was rubbing my back. Then, I turned to her and said, 'It's your turn now,' as I prepared to give her a back rub. But first, she gave me a long, sweet, passionate kiss. I don't remember rubbing her back—only the leisurely, romantic kiss. I awoke feeling very loved and blessed and incredibly fortunate to be her lover, her soul mate."

Did that dream come from our work on Chapter One of our book, titled "Three Kisses"? I was still enjoying remembering the dream when Mary Lee whispered in my ear about working on a specific project, so I got up, got dressed, and got busy. I don't question these sudden ideas, these urgings anymore. I just get busy and act on them.

Here are some insights I'm learning more about these days:

Synchronicity—pay attention to coincidences in life. Chance encounters with others often have a deeper meaning.

We often have a pre-occupation with making our lives better—more secure, more comfortable (sometimes polluting our planet in the process.)

We can learn to perceive what was formerly an invisible type of energy. Our expectations cause our energy to affect other energy systems.

One night, I thought I was coming out of the bathroom toward the bed, when I saw Mary Lee lying there. When she started to get up, I said, "No, wait, don't get up; just scoot back and little bit, so I can crawl in." I got into bed with my back toward her and moved close, so we were spooning, something we had sometimes done to feel our closeness as we slept. Almost immediately, I awoke, with a feeling of a sweet, loving peacefulness, and I realized it had not been a dream, but another soul-joining, which seems real, is very short, and you awaken with a very positive and wonderful emotion that lingers. When I realized what had happened, I thanked her for that rare and wonderful experience.

That same afternoon, I'd just had a therapeutic massage from Ellen Born and had gone into the small bathroom to get dressed, when I looked up and noticed a picture on the small bulletin board in there. I gasped with wonder and joy! It was a picture of two little sleeping babies, in the exact same position that Mary Lee and I had been in during our soul-joining! And the caption on that picture read, "Sometimes . . . Just being there *is* enough." The timing of it stunned me, and I thanked Mary Lee again.

I asked Ellen for a copy of that picture, enlarged it, framed it, and put it on a shelf in Mary Lee's lapidary room—which is now Pat's workroom, so that whenever I'm working at that counter, I look up and see it . . . and smile. I also made other copies of it, and I gave one of them to Tina Zion; it was posted on the bulletin board in her waiting room for several months.

Once, when I began cleaning out the closet in our family room, I found boxes and boxes of choir cassette tapes from 1960s to 1990s. I also found a nondescript box of letters from Mary Lee to me early in our relationship, during the mid-'70s. What a surprise! That evening, when I went to bed, I told Mary Lee, "Goodnight again, I love you." And she flashed the bedside lamp in response! I thanked her and said, "I'm glad you're with me whenever I need you!"

Another morning, I awoke from a long dream with feelings of fear and loss of my spouse. It seemed I was a husband, and another man was seducing my wife, who was willing. I couldn't shake the dream and feelings.

Then I remembered writing in chapter five of this book about TIL, and the almost two years of the same situation and the helpless, sad, furious feelings I felt for so long. I don't want to be dwelling on that experience. Why has it come up now, so many years later?

I wept during my morning meditation, when I suddenly realized that last Tuesday was my Murdy's birthday, and I hadn't even realized it! I need to shake this sadness.

I awoke another day from a dream where I was put out because Mary Lee was with a large group of people, and they all sat down, and she hadn't saved a seat for me. I couldn't sit with her, and I felt left out and was angry at her thoughtlessness. Why this dream?

The following week, two men came to see me at separate appointments on Wednesday and Thursday: one was checking out the five windows in our home that I was going to have replaced, and the other was doing a pre-arranged energy assessment of the lights of my home, inside and outside. Each day, because of their immediate response to an answer I had given to a question they had asked me, our conversations suddenly evolved into their questions about loving spirits who were active in each of their lives, a grandfather and a brother. Both were amazed and uplifted by my sharing my experiences with Mary Lee's activity in my life from the other side. I hadn't planned to mention anything about her death, but during our conversations, each of them brought up their own experiences with someone in the spirit world, and my responses seemed to bring both of them relief and joy.

During my choir rehearsal the following Tuesday, we began to sing a new song that reminds me of my Mary Lee, ever since I first heard it last August, titled "There Is None Like You." As we sang it, she did a softer, shorter version of ringing the doorbell. I was stunned and touched; tears welled up as I left the room, knowing why she rang it. When I returned, Pete asked if there was anyone at the front door, and I answered, "No. I knew it was Mary Lee." He said he had heard the doorbell, but thought it might have been on the CD. Others heard it, too. Barb Werling, a good friend who had experienced the sudden loss of her husband, Vic just eleven months after Mary Lee's passing and had also experienced some interaction from his spirit, also knew that it was Mary Lee responding to that song. We had exchanged a look of recognition when it happened. I told the choir that she's at all of their rehearsals, because she loves the energy of this choir.

Sometime later, after a phone call to my auto insurance company which brought up the raw memory of the accident and Mary Lee's death, I was grieving again, and I asked Mary Lee and God for comfort and peace. I had a strong sense of her sitting on my lap comforting me with her arms around me, and kissing me on the top of my head. And I felt the peace descend on me.

In an e-mail to my sister Jan, I closed with:

Mary Lee continues to move the sign on top of the left speaker in the Rainbow Room, ring the doorbell, and flash the light by our bed when I go into the darkened room and I tell her, "Good night, Honey; I love you." (Same ol' same ol' —never fails to make me laugh, find tears in my eyes, and make me feel very, very cherished.)

She answered back:

Your note made me smile and laugh, Pat. Mary Lee continues to have such a special relationship with you! Love you! Jan

On March 1, 2013—I journalled: "I felt lonely for my Murdy this morning and was missing her interaction. Later, at nine a.m., she gave me three songs on the short drive home. Later, she moved the sign on the speaker. Just now, she flashed the bedside lamp when I said, 'Goodnight,' and then again, when I said, 'I love you.'

"I've promised to ask her for help if I'm in danger of making unwise or unhealthy choices tomorrow. She knows I want to learn to take responsibility for my actions and to build better habits of self-discipline. As I write this, I feel her strong, pulsing energy in my head and my face. I also felt her energy as I lay on Ellen's table, after a therapeutic massage this afternoon. My faithful love, my dear friend."

Some things began to occur that I either didn't understand (dreams?) or I ignored. I didn't realize that some important things were going to happen, and I needed to pay attention to the clues, the forewarnings. I questioned some happenings, but didn't understand that they were significant, as in the following paragraph and in the second part of this chapter.

On Thursday, March 7, I awoke with this song firmly in my mind: "Jesus Walked This Lonesome Valley" and another verse, "I must walk it by myself, Oh, nobody else can walk it for me, I have to walk it by myself." Why this sad song?

The next day I saw a bunny run out into the back yard and later under the shed. I talked to it, thanked Mary Lee for showing him (her?) to me—it brightened my day.

March 8, 2013—A while ago, while in a session with Tina, I asked Mary Lee what things she had been doing with me that I hadn't I been aware of, and she had replied, "Sitting on your lap." and "Lying on the bed with you." I then asked if she was on top of or under the covers and if her head was on my shoulder as we always used to sleep or rest together. Her response about my shoulder was, "Of course." I remember thinking that her response was somewhat dismissive and curt.

Tina mentioned to me that her spirit was less in touch with the memory of her body.

March 12—I wrote, "Tonight I felt chest pains. Stress? I've been preparing for the only rehearsal next Sunday for the mass choir (forty-eight people) preparing for a funeral. I'm making out a complicated seating chart, so members of each choir will know where to sit. Muscular pain from workout with Kate yesterday? I've been having several high blood pressure readings lately. When I went to donate blood last Saturday, they refused it, because my BP was too high: 196/77. A week ago, my family doctor was concerned about several high readings (165/77.) I was concerned, too; is it a warning to me about my future health? I'm trying not to be apprehensive."

Next day: "Strong, strong pulsing for hours when I came to bed at midnight. I finally read from five to six a.m. (no sleep yet.) I put on warmer pajamas and finally slept 'til nine-thirty a.m.—the same thing happened two nights ago; when I first lay down, I had felt a strong, somewhat fast pulse that was unrelenting. (My eating for the past few days has been fine—what's going on?)"

The following morning: "I got up to open the drapes and saw a bunny eating some seed I'd put on the ground around the feeders. I talked quietly to it as it ate. (I was pleased to see it.) It didn't run away, even though it saw me; (s)he kept eating for a while and finally hopped behind the shed. (I think there's a nest under the shed.) The next day, I saw the bunny again, twice before I left for my swim aerobics class. (It always makes me smile to see it.) I slept all night, until almost eight-thirty a.m. Less pain today."

Friday, March 15, 2013—Today I heard "No Other Love" on the radio, sung by Jo Stafford, and I remembered that when Mary Lee used to sing spontaneously with joy around our home, her voice quality sounded just like Jo Stafford, and I loved to hear it. Her singing voice sounded like that for a long time, until her compromised lungs got much worse through the passing years, and the timbre of her voice changed as a result.

I miss not hearing her sing. She always sang with such heart, even in the choirs. Some of the choir photos of her singing reflect that clearly.

Friday, March 22, 2013—I've just had an incredibly joy-filled, powerful experience with Mary Lee this evening. It was a surprise to gradually realize what was happening, and it moved me to tears, to feel her joyful response.

I had been wanting to go to Fort Wayne's Cinema Center, which shows art movies and many other types, to see *Quartet*, a movie about a retirement home for actors and opera singers. I had heard an interview with the film's director, Dustin Hoffman, who said that he actually *did* use retired musicians and opera singers from all over, and that he was amazed at their vitality, energy, clear-mindedness, skill, and joy at undertaking this project, and they went even beyond his expectations! Maggie Smith (one of our favorites) was one of the main actors.

I sat back to enjoy the music and the story, watching small groups of the characters, each one rehearsing for an upcoming production/fundraiser. As I watched, it gradually dawned on me that Mary Lee had been a great fan of opera, listening to it on the radio every week from the time she was a teenager. She knew so much more about operas and had a much greater love of that genre than I ever did. Sometimes, we would drive several hours to Indiana University in Bloomington, Indiana to see incredible productions of *Aida* or *Carmen* or Gilbert and Sullivan or *The Mikado* and then drive back home, stopping along the way for a very late meal.

I was pretty sure she was sitting right next to me in the theatre, really enjoying the whole thing. I moved my purse to the seat on my left (she almost always used to sit on my right side) and I put my hand on the armrest, so she could hold my hand as we watched. Later, as the credits started to roll, something took me by surprise—I began to see the contemporary photos with the real-life names of the women and men who had played the characters in the story . . . and right next to those, were much earlier photos of them in their prime, and listing some of the productions for which they had been famous as vocalists, instrumentalists, producers, or directors. It was stunning, and I was suddenly aware of my Mary Lee's energy strongly pulsating in my back! I realized that she was incredibly pleased at all she had been hearing and was now seeing. As the credits continued, I was moved to tears of joy at the special gift of sharing these moments with her, and I recognized her excitement by the same pulsing energy in my body, just as she often greets me as I awaken each morning.

As I drove home, still in joy-filled tears, I cast about for a good friend to call, with whom I could share this experience, someone who believes and knows that loved ones can and do interact with us, and who knew Mary Lee well and would be pleased and happy for us both.

Then, as I arrived back home, she whispered in my ear—her phrase for how she often speaks to me, which I perceive as inspired, intuitive ideas. "Hey, why not write about this in Chapter 10 of our book, to show what our life together is like now?"

Okay, sounds like a good idea to me, my sweet Babboo! . . . and Continues On . . .

> *"I Won't Last a Day without You"*
> *"I Couldn't Live without Your Love"*
> *"You Know You Love Her When You Let Her Go"*

Early in 2013, I awakened from a dream and wrote this down:

"Mary Lee's leaving on a trip. I stayed with her—on a plane—I stayed with her, and I said, "This will cost me a lot of money—but I want to be with her."

Sometime later, I journalled:

I'm discouraged and crying. I need to be comforted. I need peace. Increased hip pain? Eyesight is getting worse? Jannie hasn't been in touch for months, Joe goes months with no calls. I'm stuck with all this extra weight, no progress in trying to lose what I've gained from emotional eating during the past year. Not one, but three funerals for the Celebration Singers to sing for during the next month (Jack, a member, Bob, a former member, and Rev. Carolyn, a very dear friend and supporter of the choir.) Valentine's Day coming up . . . I want to feel peace . . . Too much to do . . . I need to hear my Murdy's comforting words. Can't stop crying.

In February, 2013, I began to be increasingly aware that my Murdy was interacting with me less often, and that when she spoke to me (through Tina) it was in a way that finally prompted me in one session to burst out angrily, "Mary Lee, you're speaking to me in a formal, even detached way, as if you're a professor and I'm one of your students. I'm not one of your students, I'm your lover! You don't speak with affection to me, I haven't felt you "holding my hands" or "kissing me on my lips" for a long time, you rarely ring the door chimes to say "hi" or "I approve of what you're doing," I haven't seen a colorful light show from you for a very long time, and I don't feel your light-hearted sense of humor anymore from what you do or say during our sessions with Tina.

Tina answered me by saying that Mary Lee was continuing to learn and progress on the other side, and that she was beginning to move away from memories of having a physical body.

She said that I needed to depend less on Mary Lee and her, and more on myself. She later told me she made that last statement as an encouragement to me, but I took it as a criticism of me, and I felt like she was scolding me. I began to be frightened that my soulmate was getting ready to move on and leave me behind.

On Sunday evening, March 17, I directed a rehearsal of a mass choir of the three choirs that Jack, one of our choir members had belonged to, for a combination Good Friday service/memorial service for him. He had belonged to both of my choirs and also his church choir. He had died in December, but had wanted to have his service closer to spring, instead of winter. During February and March, I had organized the three choirs, given each member a packet with four songs and a CD with each song, and also tracks that had each vocal part separately in one channel and the choir in the other channel, so they could each work by themselves, on their own during the next two months to learn all four songs. We put it all together with just this one two-hour rehearsal, almost two weeks before the service, and I had labeled each of their chairs with their name and part. As each song took shape, I made a recording of it that night.

Before the Good Friday evening service, I made up a large seating chart, color-coded by the four singing parts, and used it for them to find their places on the evening of the service at Jack's church. I also gave all fifty of them a copy of the CD I had edited, burned, and packaged from that recording I had made during our only rehearsal together. Inside the case, each CD listed every member of the mass choir.

Looking back on it, that service and all my communications and preparations during January through March was a source of stress for me, but it also took me away from the personal fear and stress of the situation with Mary Lee—it gave me a big, important project to work on. It also filled me with joy that Friday evening, as I surprised and pleased them as I gave each one a CD with their name on it. It was also an uplifting experience for me as I directed the choir during those four songs—they really sounded wonderful, and I had made some new friends who appreciated being able to honor Jack this way. By the way, this was the third memorial service at which my Celebration Singers choir had sung during the past five weeks!

I saw Tina on Good Friday morning (March 29) and the session was filled with many questions for Mary Lee about how things would be if (when) she moved on to a different plane of existence. I cried during most of the session. One of my questions was if Tina would still be able to hear and see Mary Lee. Tina responded that she had always been able to see Mary Lee's image clearly, but that even now, it was more difficult to make out her image, because it was more diffuse and less clear to her. She also pointed out that Mary Lee was less talkative lately.

Toward the end of the session, Tina said to me, "Pat, I don't usually say this to my clients, but I strongly suggest that you get in touch with your family doctor right away and tell her that you need a prescription for an antidepressant." She told me that I was in depression right now; I told her that I'd been feeling emotionally fragile, often on the edge of tears, and that I had awakened that morning dreading the day, instead of celebrating the new day, as I had usually done before. I called my doctor from Tina's office and set up an appointment for Monday morning.

I remember that Saturday was a blur of torment, fear, and hopelessness. Easter Sunday was pretty bad; I cried during much of the church service, and toward the end of that time, two of my friends, Thelma and Susan, came and sat on either side of me and comforted me. I believe it was probably somewhat distressing for others who were used to seeing my friendly, caring, and positive self over the past couple of years.

I saw my doctor on Monday morning and began the new prescription the next day. I began talking to Mary Lee and writing down some of the things I wanted to say to her during the next session with Tina.

On Wednesday, I had a counseling session with our minister, Rev. Barry Vennard. At one point, after I mentioned Mary Lee's promise to interact with me and her son and daughter until it was our time, he paused and then suggested to me, "But what if you came to realize that it would be more helpful for Mary Lee, and maybe even more helpful for your spiritual progress, too, for her to move on to her next, more advanced stage in the afterlife?"

I didn't respond, but I felt a stab of pain at the prospect of being separated from her in my lifetime from now on, and I thought, "Maybe that won't have to happen, 'cause she promised me, and I trusted her word, and I know she loves me dearly."

The following week in a session with Laurie Rainey Schmidt, another of my spiritual counselors, she told me that Mary Lee was very likely getting ready to move on to a realm of faster vibration, and that even if she did occasionally interact with me, it would be much more subtle, and that I might not even realize it. She probably won't be doing any more electrical things, like the lights or doorbell, or the warmth in my hands or on my lips.

Later at home, as I thought of more questions to write down, my thinking became more clear, and I wrote down other things that I wanted to say to my Murdy the next Friday when I would see Tina again. I wrote: My sweet Mary Lee, my soulmate, my love—I have lots of questions for you. I know you've been progressing and changing and learning, and I don't want to slow you down or hold you back. I need to know, are you going to be able to keep the promise you made in December, 2010, to interact with me until it's my time?

Laurie said you might be progressing on to a higher vibrational level, where it's hard for you to do electrical things, like the doorbell and flashing the lamp by our bed and holding my hands and kissing my lips.

Will you still be able to whisper in my ear?

Can you still help me to write our book?

Can you do any soul joining with me?

Can your energy gently pulse in my back when I lie down?

Can you create that sweet fragrance in that one room in our home?

Can you make a gentle breeze in the house, even if it's closed up?

Can you give me special songs on the radio?

Will Tina still be able to hear you and see you?

Can you still bring the butterflies, birds and bunnies to me?

(I'm crying as I write this.)

I don't want to lose our connection.

I will continue to feel the joy and love and thankfulness for the miracle you continue to be in my life.

When I asked Tina if she would still be able to see and hear her, Tina responded that Mary Lee's form was already not as clear as it had always been before. Mary Lee was not as talkative or humorous as earlier, and today, Mary Lee said, "I feel different." I don't think she knows exactly what's going to be happening.

I told Tina that I thought that when she made that promise two-and-a-half years ago, that she would continue to interact with Jan, Joe and me until it was our time she was going by what she knew then. Now that she's been learning and progressing, it's probably time

for her to cross over. It has *still* been a wonderful, loving miracle that she has been so present for me for these past two years and eight months!

I have come to realize that her active presence has given me a sense of peace, love, and joy that has gradually become my way of life, and that I'm much stronger now than I was even a few months ago. I feel confident that I can now live my life without needing that loving crutch she has provided to me for so long, in order to help me build a richer, joy-filled life of my own for now, and throughout the future.

Then in late April, I wrote in my journal: It looks like I need to release her for the second time, just like I released her years ago, when her body was dying in the hospital.

At my last session with Tina, I told my Murdy that I hoped she'd still be in my life somehow, and that I would take her any way I could get her. When I told her I would no longer *expect* her to do the interactions she'd been doing for so long, she immediately replied, "Well, *that's* a relief!" Tina and I both laughed, because that relieved response from her really sounded like my Mary Lee, and her sense of humor, which I had been missing for the past few months!

But I also told her that because I love her so much, I didn't want to try to hold her here or slow her progress or postpone this next phase of her journey. It's kind of like what I told her at the hospital earlier: "I don't know what I'll do without you . . . but I'll be okay."

I'm learning to trust in God's highest good for me, whatever it is.

My sister Jan sent this e-mail to me: "When it comes to Mary Lee, I read what you said about her changing. That is just further proof to me that all of this (about the spirit world) is true, because the definition of *life* is *change*. Nothing that lives remains static—only dead things remain the same. Problem is, I sometimes don't *like* change; I get comfortable with the way things are and want to relax and just enjoy it. But God wants me to *grow* and that means I have to change. So-o-o, that means because Mary Lee is alive (in another realm,) she is growing and changing, too. That can be kind of scary for you, but it shouldn't be, because she gave you her promise: to stay with you until you join her in that other realm. You can trust that she will keep that promise, even though her way of showing it may change. *Your Murdy will always love you.*"

Still later, Jan wrote, "Thank you for sharing with me. I know this will be a very difficult period of letting go for you and I will continue to keep you in my prayers. You are right . . . Mary Lee's continuing participation in your life since her death had been a very precious gift not experienced by many who have lost their loved ones. You now have very unique memories of her loving, laughing presence and the firm assurance that that love will never end. You have been truly blessed!"

I've been able to be grateful for all that Mary Lee's spirit has done to help me become a stronger and happier and more loving person, and I've been able to release my need for her to move things, or flash lights, or send me songs on the radio so we both can move on.

A *big* spiritual step for me.

Uh—wait a minute; what's going on now??

To my knowledge, Mary Lee hasn't interacted with me for about a month and a half, and I'm okay. I'm convinced that back in March, she whispered in Ray's ear (one of my really spiritually aware choir members) to leave me that funny solar-powered hula bunny on the large window sill of the Rainbow Room at the end of our last rehearsal of the season on March 19, 2013. And a day or so later, he also brought me a cute little baby chickie that also did a fast hula when the sun shone on it; I put that one on the large ledge of the bay window in our bedroom. Every time I see it

moving in that room, I smile or chuckle. Every day, as I open the drapes, its dancing begins my mornings with happiness, and it reminds me of her sense of humor and her love. (. . . and also, that she sometimes whispers in the receptive ears of others, too.)

On May 16, 2013, several things happened that gave me an incredible and touching surprise . . .

The previous summer I had attended a sightreading session where many, many choir directors like me were reading through more than eighty newly published songs, in hopes of finding some new songs for our choirs. When the song "There Is None Like You" began, I immediately sensed from the lyrics that the song was about my Mary Lee! Later, I realized that she gave it to me at that time. I was so touched by the words that I got choked up, and couldn't even sing it. I took my copy home, thinking it was a song just for me, not for my choir.

Gradually, I changed my mind, removed a hymn that was in the middle of it, fixed the accompaniment CD the same way, and presented it to my Celebration Singers choir, telling them about how it had deeply touched me and reminded me of someone I loved very much. Of course, they all knew it was Mary Lee. I asked them to "think of someone in your life that you dearly love, who loves you back, and remember them as you sing the song. It could be someone younger or older than you, they could still be present in your life or it could be from the past, or they might not even be physically here anymore. Just think of them every time you sing this song, and dedicate it to them." Several choir members found it difficult to sing, just like it had been for me; we all had to take some time to process the emotions it brought up in each of us. Now, when we sing this for a performance, I tell the audience the same thing I'd previously said to the choir members. Sometimes, it even brings tears to some in the audience. So this is Mary Lee's song.

I had decided to make a special CD of that song for John, a new friend I got to know during the pastor's class we both attended for several months. After my choir had sung that song for our worship service recently, he had asked me, "How could you sing that song without crying?" He understood the significance of the song to me. He expressed an interest in seeing the song, and I planned to make him a CD of it.

I went into the Rainbow Room to work on the CD. I turned on the right speaker, and as I walked toward the left speaker, I noticed that the sign perched on top of it was sitting exactly where it was supposed to be. Previously, she had often moved the sign in various ways, while I was sitting with my back to it as I worked on making choir recordings. When I'd finished my work and turned around, I was always surprised and delighted every time I saw that she had moved it.

About two years earlier, as I was also preparing to record a song she had previously given me titled "There Is None Like You," she hadn't moved that sign for nine months—since the previous April, when she had crossed over, moving on to another realm. She hadn't been interacting with me in any way for about three months, since I had released her to go on, just like I'd previously released her at the hospital two years and eight months earlier.

As I turned on the left speaker, I remember saying to her, "I know you won't be moving this sign anymore . . . and that's okay." Then, when I had finished making that CD, I stood up, turned around and started to walk toward the left speaker. I was astounded to see that she had turned the sign 180 degrees!

I tearfully laughed and said, "I didn't think you could do that anymore! I love you, sweetheart!" Then, on my way to class, she gave me these songs on the car radio, one after the other. She hadn't done that since the end of March!

"Last Dance (tonight")—Donna Summer
"May All of Your Days Be a Good Day"—Andy Williams
"I Love, Love, Love You in So Many Ways"

"Precious and Few Are the Moments We Two Can Share"
"You're One in a Million"
"You Are My Shining Star" (just as I arrived at the church)

It was a blitzkrieg of love and connections, from three or four p.m. to nine p.m. on that day! Wow!

The next morning, as I drove to Laurie's office . . . from the time I started my car in the garage, until I was parking at Laurie's, Mary Lee had given me seven more songs. The last one was John Denver singing "My Sweet Lady," which had been the very first song she had sent me two years ago, with the words saying again that our time together had only begun.

I didn't understand what was happening, but I felt as though she was assuring me that she's still aware of what's going on in my life. Tina had begun teaching me about what was happening . . .

Spirits who have passed over and have gone on to a higher level can sometimes quickly come and go—can easily project themselves back here. Pop in and out and briefly interact when they choose to.

I asked Tina, "Is it unusual for a spirit to stick around for two years and eight months?"

She responded, "No, sometimes they stay for hundreds of years, usually in their home, and usually because they are really attached to something they like—furniture, silverware, etc."

I asked, "But do they remain attached that long for another person?"

Tina replied that no, she hasn't heard of that.

So Mary Lee's soul really *did* do something extraordinary by staying with me for so long because of her incredible love for me, and so she could help me through my grief and my dependence on her presence. Tina explained, "Mary Lee stayed until you were ready for her to go. *She* knew that you were ready, but she waited until *you* knew that you were ready."

When I realized how much stronger and more secure I was now, than I was even a couple of months ago, I knew that I had indeed found my own joy in life, and had gradually learned to live securely and peacefully without needing her physical presence.

When I released her that second time, I had asked her if she would say good-bye to me in a way that I would recognize, so that I'd know when she was leaving to move on, and she did exactly that . . . although at the time, I didn't recognize it as her good-bye for now.

At that time, she hadn't been interacting with me (by moving things or ringing the doorbell or flashing a lamp before I'd even touched it,) for a month and a half, but then . . . three nights in a row, she flashed the bedside lamp in the darkened room as I told her goodnight. And in the middle of the last night, when I went into the bathroom, she lit up the whole bathroom with the normally dim, flickering nightlight over the sink, making it suddenly as bright as a spotlight. I was amazed and said, "Was that you, Mary Lee?!" She responded by doing it a second time, even brighter! I laughed and said, "You're a corker, Mary Lee; I really love you!" as I crawled back into bed and promptly returned to a peaceful sleep.

It was only a few days later, when there were again no more interactions, that I finally realized that those special things had been her message of "I'm going now," to me . . . and it was okay. I was okay.

Epilogue
What's in Our Future?

"If Ever You're in My Arms Again"
"There'll Never Be Anyone Else for Me but You"

On May 21, 2013, Mary Lee was there to protect me from serious injury and possible death in a seventy-plus mph full force, violent rear-end collision when my car, a Prius, was totaled by a very large van, but I was not. She has since taken part in many kinds of healing sessions with spiritually aware professionals who are aware of her healing presence, her love and protection, and even occasionally, her sense of humor.

She continues to whisper in my ear to bring me the spiritual understanding and the growth and transformation I continue to seek in my life—and I've learned to pay attention to sudden insights and new ideas, and I thank her when they come to me.

I've also continued to keep a small notebook I began in March, 2011 which is titled, "Look for chances to lighten someone's load."

By the way, remember that life-changing journey I made to Elko, Nevada in July, 2011? Now, two years later in July, 2013, that experience blossomed out into a very large Deihl Family Reunion, with almost everyone—forty-seven extended family members. Most attended for more than two days of activities and enthusiastic, positive conversations among many people who had never met, or who hadn't seen one another in fifteen to thirty years! Our generation had gone from having the eight little kids who saw one another every year at Christmas celebrations to being the oldest generation, who were now grandparents or even great-grandparents—four generations of us, from seven months old to mid-eighties years old!

Such positive energy was evident each time we met together, in small and large groups that weekend! And yes, we did take pictures—which included having a chair right next to me, labelled with a sign: "Mary Lee Richeson, here in spirit." We also made another sign for "Margie and Larry Waite," my youngest sister and her husband, who couldn't travel at that time because of health issues.

Some of us were in both pictures, others in one or the other, due to flight conditions, jobs, and a car race entered by three of my Elko family members and attended by some out-of-town family members.

Later, I shipped a framed, 10 x 12 copy of the two large group pictures to each family of each generation, so that everyone would have something to remember one another by, and that weekend together. Several family members asked me to be sure to label it with the names of everyone.

It finally dawned on me, that I was the only one who knew all their names, because Mary Lee and I had kept in touch with them all, throughout the years.

Since then, many of these new connections have continued, with one of my nephews recently actually moving across the country to the city where one of my nieces and her family have lived for years, and mini-reunions are recurring with members who now have more awareness and appreciation of our extended family. We also will begin plans for our next large reunion, perhaps in a year or two.

And babies continue to be born. In Mary Lee's family, young Owen Richeson, Mary Lee's first great grandson, was born to Paul and Sara Richeson on . . . are you ready for this? Owen's birthday celebration will be every July 31st, which was actually the date of that terrible car/truck accident in 2010. But now, that date signifies something wonderful— the birth of a sweet new soul on this earth. Ain't Divine Order grand? Who says God doesn't have a sense of humor?

POWERFUL MIRACLES STILL DO HAPPEN

On a Friday in November 2014 (the day after Thanksgiving,) I received a call from Larry, my brother-in-law and Margie's husband. He said that two-year-old Ryan, their youngest grandchild, had been found lying on the bottom of their pool at their Texas home. They didn't know how long he'd been there.

He was rushed to the ICU of the Children's Hospital in Dallas; he had no brain waves, and he was non-responsive. The neurologist told his parents, Jon and Martha, that they needed to tell his family to fly there right away to see Ryan for the last time.

I was inconsolable, grieving his impending death as I began thinking of him in the past tense: he was such a sweet little kid, with his boundless energy and his shy smile.

Later, Larry called me again, saying that the next morning, he would be taking the 6:40 am flight to Dallas. I didn't know who else would be going, but I knew I couldn't make the trip physically, and my choir also had almost a dozen Christmas concerts scheduled in the next two weeks which I had to direct. I felt torn that I couldn't go, too.

As it turned out, my e-mail became the conduit whereby Larry or Jon or Margie would give me each update, and I would pass them on to groups already in my address book—all of the Deihl family, much of Mary Lee's family, both of my choirs, my church, two of my healers, and my personal trainer, Kate. I asked them all for prayers for Ryan and his family, and many of them enlisted their church congregations to pray for him, too. Silent Unity (in Missouri) was holding him in prayer for the next thirty days, also. This is a 24/7, day/night prayer support ministry that has been going on in Unity for over a century. (1/800/669-7729)

Ryan had already been put on a respirator, and the doctors induced a coma to give his body a chance to heal. They said that even if he survived, he would probably be brain damaged from the extended time without oxygen.

I asked Margie to impress on all of the adults that they needed to talk to Ryan, to tell him how much they loved him and

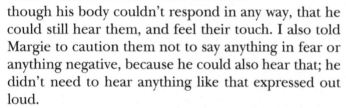

Brothers Devin, Ryan, and Lucas

wanted him to be well. I said that even though his body couldn't respond in any way, that he could still hear them, and feel their touch. I also told Margie to caution them not to say anything in fear or anything negative, because he could also hear that; he didn't need to hear anything like that expressed out loud.

By Sunday morning on the third day, the doctors said they would very slowly begin raising his temperature, so that just maybe he might wake up from the coma. And he did begin to! They had to give him a slight sedative, so he wouldn't fight to pull out the tubes in him. He finally opened his eyes and was alert, as he watched whoever was talking. They removed the tubes so they could take MRIs of his brain and his lungs. Later Sunday evening, the doctors looked at all the many pictures and declared that all of the MRIs were absolutely normal! He had no damage to his brain *or* to his lungs!

The neurologist, who had thought there was no hope for recovery, now exclaimed that it was a miracle! The nurse who saw the pictures also said, "It's a miracle!" His two young cousins from Indiana, Samantha and Nathan, finally came in to see him, now that all the tubes were gone and he was awake. When he saw his older brothers enter his room, he grinned

and tried to sit up. Larry had later remarked, "*Now* I believe in miracles."

Margie said that before she and Larry left for their hotel that evening, Martha was on the bed, holding Ryan in her arms. By this time, the only thing Ryan had hooked up to him was an IV, delivering medicine to cure his strep throat infection. He complained about the bandage on his thumb, because that was the thumb he sometimes sucked. So, they moved it to the other thumb, and he was a happy little boy again.

Larry soon wrote me an e-mail, thanking me for all of my help. "Good thing you stayed home. You were in the right place at the right time." I had been forwarding each update to everyone, and spared Ryan's parents and grandparents from having to spend time and energy on those communications to everyone.

Such a remarkable outcome from such a tragedy has surely strengthened many people's faith and belief in miracles. Tina Zion, my grief counselor, wrote: "Oh, my goodness Pat—I am tearing up as I read this last update. There was actually an article in the *USA Today* newspaper about some scientific studies regarding the power of prayer, and that all the studies showed that it makes a huge difference; I was part of the thousands who were praying for Ryan."

And I was one of many who journeyed during a very brief time, from helplessness and hopelessness to a stronger faith and a firm belief in the power of prayer . . . and *big* miracles!

Almost a week later, I learned that Martha was the one who found her youngest son in the pool; she jumped in and almost went into shock from the icy-cold water. She couldn't lift Ryan out of the pool, and she called for her oldest son, eight-year old Devin, to help her. He immediately ran out, grabbed his little brother and heaved him out of the pool. Then, he ran into the house and dialed 911 for an ambulance.

WHAT A HERO! He saved his little brother's life! Thank you, Devin . . . and courageous Martha!

"My Heart Will Go On" (Celine Dion)

I've left up the welcome sign by the front porch that Jannie gave us years ago, since even now, my Mary Lee abides in our home. I still enjoy wearing her pajamas and many of her other clothes, and much of the jewelry she had made in the lapidary. It still makes me laugh when she moves something, such as turning the little hula chickie that dances in the sun on our bedroom windowsill, so that it's back is to me when I open the drapes, or it's been moved much closer to the front of the windowsill.

If I were to attempt to sum up the wonderful results of our thirty-six years together, I believe that the following song "Because I Knew You . . . I have been changed for good" from the musical *Wicked* would describe it best.

One Sunday morning, when our soloist and our good friend, Michel Holland sang this song, Mary Lee and I sat close in our pew (near the front) holding hands, with tears in our eyes, because we both felt that these lyrics perfectly described how we both felt about our relationship.

These lyrics are so perfect for us and maybe also for some of you?

I am an alumna of Wittenberg University, where I earned my first advanced degree.

Wittenberg has the following motto, and I've always remembered and often quoted it:

"Having light, we pass it on to others"

My hope is that many of you who have read this book have received some new light in your lives, in the form of new hope, peace, joy, faith, love, and a new and maybe growing discovery and knowledge of a very important part of yourself that *all* of us really *do* possess:

A new awareness and acknowledgement of that spiritual part of us, and a willingness to get to know our own souls.

The best love is the kind that awakens the soul,
and makes us reach for more,
that plants a fire in our hearts
and brings peace to our minds . . .

Years ago, Mary Lee and I were both extremely moved by a touching, dramatic scene at the end of the fourth season of the TV show, *Xena, Warrior Princess* in the Episode titled "The Ides of March."

In the story, Xena and her soulmate, Gabrielle were being crucified by the Roman soldiers.

As they were being nailed onto the crosses, even through their pain, they declared their love for each other. Later, when their bodies had finally died . . . something incredible happened.

A beautiful, glorified Xena (her soul/spirit) emerged from her beaten and tortured physical body, looked over at Gabrielle's dead body on the other cross, and floated over in front of her.

Holding Gabrielle's face gently in her hands, she roused her soul from her body; they held hands as they turned away from the crosses and they moved quickly out into space to begin their spiritual journey together. Mary Lee and I had been sitting close together and were also holding hands as we watched all this. We wept at the wonder and beauty of how it had ended, as we gazed into each other's eyes.

Some years earlier, Mary Lee and I had heard a beautiful song of love that had also brought tears to our eyes, especially as we heard how the song ended.

It seems fitting to share with all of you the lyrics of that song, as we complete this book which has shared our story with you.

"If"
(Bread - sung by David Gates)

If a picture paints a thousand words, then why can't I paint you?
The words will never show the "you" I've come to know.
If a face could launch a thousand ships, then where am I to go?
There's no one home but you, you're all that's left me, too.
And when my love for life is running dry,
you come and pour yourself on me.

And if I could be two places at one time, I'd be with you.
Tomorrow and today, beside you all the way.
If the world should stop revolving, spinning slowly down to die,
I'd spend the end with you . . . and when the world was through,
then one by one, the stars would all go out,
and you and I . . . would simply fly . . . away.

Um . . . we couldn't resist.
She made me do it!

The End!

ABOUT THE AUTHOR, PAT DEIHL

Pat Deihl was at the 2012 Xena, Warrior Princess Convention in Burbank, California giving away more than two large tables and a clothing rack full of Xena memorabilia (including luggage, jewelry, jackets, sweaters, and t-shirts, many boxes of fan fiction, DVDs, videotapes, mugs, and many posters) in memory of her soul mate and life partner Mary Lee Richeson, who had passed on in early September, 2010.

Then, when her tables were virtually empty, the people at the neighboring table remarked, "You need to tell your story; you need to write a book about you and Mary Lee."

Pat answered, "I'm not a professional writer; I can't do that." Claudia Wilde, from Bedazzled Ink Publishing Company, responded, "We'll help you." They planted the seed and now, here we are, completing that book.

Pat was born in 1939 in Indiana, and she began piano lessons when she was eight years old. Music was destined to be her life. She began singing in her church choir at age ten; by the time she was in seventh grade, when she began accompanying the junior high school choir there, she knew she wanted to be a high school choir director. She sang in and accompanied choirs throughout high school and college.

Pat earned her Bachelor of Science in Music Education degree in 1961 from Wittenberg University at Springfield, Ohio. She received her Master's Degree in Music Education in 1967 from Indiana University on the Bloomington Campus. She taught music (and choirs) for thirty-four years in public schools, from grade school, junior high school, and eventually high school. For years, Pat was also the choir director/music director at her church.

When she retired from teaching in 1995, she had already created an adult community choir, The Celebration Singers, which continues to be extremely active today, and also became the director of another adult choir, The Festival Choir, which consisted of choir directors and choir members from about twenty different churches in the Fort Wayne area. The first choir has sung together for twenty-two years, mostly in retirement and nursing homes; the other choir has performed primarily in churches (including three trips to Europe) for thirty years. Since Pat began to be their director twenty years ago, the choir also has had a prison ministry. Her choirs are still her passion and her joy in life.

Pat's other passion and joy in life is her Mary Lee, who sang in each of Pat's choirs and loved Pat as no other had.

They began their shared lives at ages thirty-five and fifty, in the year 1975. Thus, the title of this book: We Came Alive in '75! aptly describes how their long and rich union positively affected both of them over the span of their incredible thirty-six years together.

If you'd like to give Pat some comments/feedback, share a personal spiritual experience you've had, or ask her a question or two, you can e-mail her at: wecamealive@comcast.net or send a message to her through Bedazzled Ink at: editor@bedazzledink.com.

Songs My Mary Lee Has Given Me since 2011

This became one important and effective way she connects to me

> *"I Have to Say 'I Love You' in a Song"*

(Use your computer to find lyrics and performances of any song.)

As I listened to the radio (mostly in my car) or to music in a restaurant . . . or my swim aerobics class, some of these songs Mary Lee was "singing" to me, some were of me "singing" to her, and most were about both of us and our relationship.

"After the Lovin' . . . I'm still in love with you" (Englebert Humperdink)

"Afternoon Delight" (the Starlight Vocal Band)

"Ain't No Mountain High Enough . . . If you need me, call my name, and I'll be there (Diana Ross)

"Ain't No Woman Like the One I Got" (Four Tops)

"Along Comes Mary . . ." (The Association)

"Always" (Paul McCartney)

"All I Know" (Art Garfunkel)

"All the Way" (Frank Sinatra)

"And I Love Her" (The Beatles, Harry Connick, Jr)

"And I Love You So" (Perry Como)

"At the End of a Rainbow, our love will go on 'til the end of time" (Nat King Cole).

"Beauty and the Beast" (Celine Dion, Peabo Bryson)

"Because I Knew You . . . I have been changed for good" (from the musical Wicked)

This speaks of being brought together to learn something, to grow —if we allow it, and that knowing you has changed me, made me who I am today. I think the lyrics really resonate for both of us.

"Because of You" (Tony Bennett)

"Because You Love Me" (Celine Dion)

Great words!

"Bewitched, Bothered and Bewildered" (Carly Simon)

"Blue Moon" (Ella Fitzgerald)

"Bridge over Troubled Water" (Art Garfunkrl

"But Beautiful" (Gordon Lightfoot)

"Can You Feel the Love Tonight" (Lion King) (Elton John)

"Canadian Sunset" (Andy Williams)

"Can't Get Used to Losin' You, gonna live my whole life through loving you." (Andy Williams)

"Can't Help Falling in Love with You" (Elvis)

"Can't Help Myself, I Fall in Love with You" (Anne Murray)

"Catch a Falling Star" (Perry Como)

"Celebration!" (Kool & the Gang)

"Chances Are" (Johnny Mathis)

"Cherish the Life We Live" (Kool and The Gang)

Especially the chorus!

"Close to You" (Carpenters)

"Come Away with Me" (Norah Jones)

"Could I Have This Dance" (Anne Murray)

Great lyrics!

We once took up a challenge to sing a song for the crowd at a Xena Convention, in order to win a prize, so we stood up and sang this whole song from memory and won a great DVD! I think many others who were there love this song, too!

We always requested this song at any dance. In 2000, it was our "first dance" at our wedding reception. In 2010, I had them play it just before I spoke at Mary Lee's memorial service. Be sure to check out the lyrics, if you don't already know and love this song!

"Darling, Je Vous Aime Beaucoup (Nat Cole)
"Devoted To You" (Everley Brothers)
"Do That to Me One More Time" (Captain and Tennille)
"Do You Want to Know a Secret" (The Beatles)
It speaks of "whispering in your ear" as Mary Lee calls it.
"Don't You Know" (Della Reese)
"Elusive Butterfly" (Bob Lind)
Learning to pay attention to and trust imagination and intuition.
"Evergreen" (Barbra Streisand)
Great Words! What a romantic love song.
"Everybody Loves Somebody Sometime" (Dean Martin)
"For All We Know" (the Carpenters)
"For Once in My Life" (Stevie Wonder)
"Friendly Persuasion" (Pat Boone)
"Georgy Girl" (The Seekers)
This song connects with my physical and inner transformation, when we began.
. . . there's another Pat (Georgy) deep inside . . .
"Give Me the Simple Life" (Tony Bennett)
"Goin' to the Chapel and We're Gonna Get Married" (The Dixie Cups)
"Gone Too Soon" (Michael Jackson)
The first time I heard this, I didn't know the song, or who was singing it.
I was on my way to my church, and the impact of the music and words blindsided me. Grief swept over me, tears ran down my cheeks, and I pulled into the parking lot to listen to it until it ended. When I heard it again some weeks later, I was astonished to learnit was not a woman with a beautiful, fragile voice, but rather Michael Jackson.
"The Greatest Love of All" (Whitney Houston)
"The Greatest Thing . . . you'll ever learn is just to love, and be loved in return—Nature Boy" (Nat King Cole)
"Have I Told You Lately That I Love You" (Rod Stewart)
"Have to Believe We Are Magic" (Olivia Newton John)
"Have You Never Been Mellow?" (Olivia Newton John)
"Heaven Must Be Missing an Angel" (Tavares)
"Hold Me, Hold Me" (Mel Carter)
"Honey, I Miss You" (Bobby Goldsboro)
"Hopelessly Devoted to You" (Olivia Newton John)
"How Deep Is Your Love" (Bee Gees)
We disco danced to this in the '70s!
"How Sweet It Is To Be Loved by You" (James Taylor)

"I Believe in Angels" (ABBA)
"I Can Only Give You Love That Lasts Forever . . . that's all" (Rod Stewart)
"I Can See Clearly Now" (Johnny Nash)
"I Couldn't Live without Your Love" (Petula Clark)
"I Dreamed a Dream" (from "Les Miz") (Susan Boyle)
"I Feel Like Makin' Love to You" (Roberta Flack)
"I Feel the Earth Move under My Feet" (Carole King)
"I Honestly Love You" (Olivia Newton John)
"I Just Can't Help Believing'" (BJ Thomas)
"I Just Called to Say I Love You" (Stevie Wonder)
"I Just Fall in Love Again" (Dreamin'(Anne Murray)
Wonderful words.
"I Know I'll Never Find Another You" (The Seekers)
"I Love a Rainy Night" (Eddie Rabbit)
"I Love How You Love Me" (Bobby Vinton)
"I Love You More Than I Can Say" (Leo Sayer)
"I Love You More Today than Yesterday, but not as much as tomorrow" (Spiral Staircase)
"I Never Wanted to Love a Man...The Way That I Want to Love You" (Captain and Tennille)
The third time she gave me this song, I finally realized the double meaning of the words for me!
"I Never Knew Love Before" (The Spinners)
"I Only Have Eyes for You" (The Flamingos)
"I Only Want to Be with You" (Dusty Springfield)
"I Wanna Hold Your Hand" (The Beatles)
"I Want To Sing You a Love Song" (Anne Murray)
"I Will Always Love You" (Whitney Houston)
"I Won't Last a Day without You" (The Carpenters)
"I Would Give Anything I Own" (Dave Gates & Bread)
Great words.
"I Write the Songs" (Barry Manilow)
"If" (Bread – David Gates)
"If Ever You're in My Arms Again . . . this time, I'll love you much better " (Peabo Bryson)
"If I Loved You" (from *Carousel* by Rodgers and Hammerstein) (Robert Goulet)
"If I May" (Nat King Cole)
"If It Takes Forever, I Will Wait for You" (Connie Francis)
"If Not for You" (Olivia Newton John)
"If Only My Love Was Here" (Paul McCartney)
"If You Leave Me Now, You Take Away the Biggest Part of Me" (Chicago)

"I'll Be Your Friend, and Your Lover" (Gloria Loring and Carl Anderson)

"I'm Happy Just to Be with You" (Anne Murray)

"I'm Hooked on a Feeling" (BJ Thomas)

"In the Misty Moonlight" (Dean Martin)

"It Could've Been Anyone at All" (Carole King)

"It Had to Be You" (Harry Connick, Jr.)

"It's a New Day, It's a New Life for me....and I'm Feelin' Good" (Michael Buble)

"It's Good to Be Back Home Again" (John Denver)

"It's My Happy, Happy Heart" (Andy Williams)

"It's Too Late to Turn Back Now" (Cornelius Bros.)

"It's Wonderful, Wonderful" (Johnny Mathis)

"I've Got the World on a String" (Frank Sinatra)

"Just An Old-Fashioned Love Song" (Three Dog Night)

"Just in Time" (Dean Martin)

"Just My Imagination" (The Temptations)

"Just You and I" (Eddie Rabbit and Crystal Gayle)

"Killing Me Softly" (Roberta Flack)

"Kisses Sweeter than Wine" (Jimmie Rodgers)

"The Lady in Red" (Chris de Burgh)

"Last Dance" (Donna Summer)

"Lean on Me" (Bill Withers)

"Let Me Be There" (Olivia Newton John)

"Let There Be Love" (Nat King Cole)

"Like a Prayer" (Madonna)

"The Lion Sleeps Tonight" (the Tokens)

"The Look of Love" (Sergio Mendez-Brazil 66)

"Love Is in the Air" (John Paul Young)

"Love Lifted Me" with additional words by Kenny Rogers (*neat arrangement*)

"A Love Like Yours surely come my way" (Everyday) (James Taylor)

"Love Me with All Your Heart" (Ray Charles Singers)

"Love Was Made For Me and You" (Nat King Cole)

"Magic Moments" (Perry Como)

"Masterpiece – Mary Lee and Pat" (Larry Heral composed this especially for us.)

"May All of Your Days Be a Good Day" (Andy Williams)

"Merry Christmas Darlin'" (Vanessa Williams)

"Midnight Train to Georgia' (Gladys Knight)

"Misty" (Johnny Mathis)

"Moon River" (by Henry Mancini) (Andy Williams)

"More Than a Woman To Me" (Bee Gees)

We disco danced to this one!

"My Endless Love" (Lionel Richie and Diana Ross)

"My Heart Belongs to Me" (Barbra Streisand)

"My Heart Belongs to Only You" (Bobby Vinton)

"My Heart Stood Still" (Rod Stewart)

"My Heart Will Go On"(from *Titanic*) (Celine Dion)

"My Lady Love" (Lou Rawls)

"My Love Does It Good" (Paul McCartney)

"My love has no beginning, my love has no end" (Nancy Wilson)

"My One and Only Love" (Nancy Wilson)

"My Prayer" (The Platters)

"My Sweet Lady" (John Denver))

Be sure to check out these words!

Early in 2011, this song was the first of her messages to me through song. Much later, it was her last "reconnecting song on May 18, 2013, after I'd "released" her a second time, when she needed to "cross over."

At the beginning, it's about my tears, my grief that our time together was finished and assures me she's close to me and that our time together is only beginning. As it played, I wept, as I realized it was a clear, healing message to me. She still sends me songs today!

"My Valentine" (Paul McCartney)

"Never Knew Love Like This Before" (Stephanie Mills)

"Never My Love" (The Association))

(Take It) "Nice and Easy" (Barbra Streisand)

"No Other Love" (Jo Stafford) – melody by Chopin

Mary Lee often sang around the house, and to me, her voice sounded just like Jo Stafford!

"No Sugar for Me Tonight" (The Guess Who)

Just as I started my car to go home after a counseling session where I had just expressed my determination to stop my "emotional eating," to cut out sugar, this song came on, repeating and repeating the title; I burst out laughing at her encouragement and sense of humor!

"Oh, How Happy You Have Made Me" (Shades of Blue)

"Oh, What a Night!" (The Four Seasons)

"On the Sunny Side of the Street" (Ella Fitzgerald)

"One Moment in Time" (Whitney Houston)

"One of a Kind Love Affair" (The Spinners)

"Only Our Hearts Will Know" (Paul McCartney)

"Only Yesterday" (Karen Carpenter)

"Our Love Is Here To Stay" (Natalie Cole) (Ella Fitzgerald)

"Peace Train" (Cat Stevens)

"Pina Colada Song" (in a rut?) (Rupert Holmes)

"Please Love Me Forever" (Bobby Vinton)

"Precious and Few Are the Moments We Two Can Share" (1972-*Climax*)

"Precious Moments" (Diana Ross)

"Pretty Woman" (Roy Orbison)

"Pure Imagination" (from *Willy Wonka and the Chocolate Factory*)

This song is about learning to "see" and "hear" her – to pay attention and use my imagination.

"Put a Little Love in Your Heart" (Jackie DeShannon)

"Put Your Head on My Shoulder" (the Lettermen) *She "whispers in my ear" now.*

"Remember the Times of Your Life" (Paul Anka)

"The Rose" (Bette Midler)

"Save the Best for Last" (Vanessa Williams)

"Savin' All My Love for You" (Whitney Houston)

"She Believes in Me" (Kenny Rogers)

"She Loves Me Like a Rock" (Paul Simon)

"She's a Lady" (Tom Jones)

"Silly Love Songs" (Paul McCartney"

"Sing" (the Carpenters)

"So Far Away" (Carole King)

Sometimes, I still mourn the loss of her physical presence.

"So I Have to Say I Love You in a Song" (Jim Croce)

"Someday"(The Lettermen)

"Someone to Watch over Me" (Linda Ronstadt)

"Something Tells Me I'm into Something Good" (Herman's Hermits)

"Somewhere" (from *West Side Story*) (Barbra Streisand)

"Somewhere Down the Road" (Barry Manilow) *(Very touching words, with a much deeper meaning)*

"Somewhere in the Night" (Barry Manilow)

"Somewhere, Out There" (James Ingram)

"Stand by Me" (Ben E. King)

"Stayin' Alive" (The Bee Gees)

We disco danced to this one.

"Still the One" (Orleans)

"Suddenly" (Billy Ocean)

"Sukiyaki" (English translation) (Taste of Honey)

"Sunny, Thank You for..." (Bobby Hebb)

"Sweet Caroline" (Neil Diamond)

When we heard this, I always sang to her, "Sweet Mary Lee"!

"Sweet, Sweet Memories You Gave-a Me" (Dean Martin)

"S' Wonderful" (Diana Krall)

"Tenderly" (Nat "King" Cole)

"Thank You for Being My Wife" (Al Martino)

When he was dying, this is one of the songs he recorded, to give his wife an income after he was gone.

"Thank You for the Music" (ABBA) (Ch. 10)

"That Holiday Feelin'" (Steve and Edie Gorme)

I decided not to write about it, but not very long after Mary Lee's passing, a good friend from high school days asked if she could kiss me on the lips; I was stunned by her request and said "No." Soon after, when I started my car, this song came on the radio in mid-song, and I heard: "...I bet your lips are warm and sweet" and I burst out laughing!

"That's All" (Nat King Cole)

Sweet words.

"That's What Friends Are For" (Stevie Wonder, Elton John, Dionne Warwick)

"The More I See You" (Chris Montez)

(I've had) The "Time of My Life" (Dirty Dancing) (Bill Medley, Jennifer Warnes)

"Then Came You"

"There Is None Like You" (The Celebration Singers)

From the day I first sight-read this song, I knew it was about my Mary Lee, and that she had "given" it to me.

"There, I've Said It Again" (Bobby Vinton)

"There'll Never Be Anyone Else for Me But You" (Rick Nelson)

"This Is My Song (Petula Clark)

"This Time the Girl Is Gonna Stay" (BJ Thomas)

"Three Times a Lady" (Lionel Richie)

Thoughtful and loving words.

"Through the Years" (Kenny Rogers)

"Time After Time" (Margaret Whiting)

"Time in a Bottle" (Jim Croce)

"To the Ends of the Earth" (Nat "King" Cole)

"Today" (New Christy Minstrels)

"Torn Between Two Lovers" (Mary MacGregor)

"Truly" (Lionel Richie)

"Unchained Melody" (the Righteous Brothers)

"Unforgettable" (Natalie and Nat "King" Cole)

"Until the 12th of Never" (Johnny Mathis)

"Up Where We Belong" (Joe Cocker, Jennifer Lawrence)

Especially check out the words in the verse that begins: "Some hang on to yesterday . . ."

"The Wedding Song" (Paul Stookey, of Peter, Paul and Mary)

"We're in This Love Together" (Al Jarreau)

"We've Got a Groovy Kind of Love" (Phil Collins)

"We've Only Just Begun" (The Carpenters)

"What a Wonderful World' (Louis Armstrong)

"What Will My Mary Say? (Johnny Mathis)

See "That Holiday Feeling" – same story.

"What's Forever For?" (Michael Murphy)

"When I Am with You" (Johnny Mathis)

"When I Fall in Love"(Natalie and Nat King Cole)

"When I Need You" (Leo Sayer)

"When Will I See You Again?" ("Precious Moments") (The Three Degrees)

"When You Wish upon a Star" (Cliff Edwards)

"When Will I Hold/see/touch You Again?" ("Weekend in New England") (Barry Manilow)

"Where Do I Begin?" (Andy Williams)

"Wherever you go, my heart will go, too" (Vic Damone)

"Whither Thou Goest" (Jan Richeson Davis)

"Who Knows Where or When" (The Lettermen)

"A Whole New World" (Peabo Bryson and Regina Belle)

"The Wind Beneath My Wings" (Bette Midler)

"Wish We Didn't Have to Meet . . . Secretly" (1958-Jimmie Rodgers)

"With You, I'm Born Again" (Billy Preston and Syreeta Wright)

Great words!

(I am) "A Woman in Love" (Barbra Streisand)

"The Wonder of You" (Elvis Presley)

"Wonderful, Wonderful" (Johnny Mathis)

"Yesterday's Songs" (Neil Diamond)

"You Are the Sunshine of My Life" (Stevie Wonder)

"You Belong to Me" (Carly Simon)

"You Could've Been Anyone At All" (Carole King)

"You Decorated My Life" (Kenny Rogers)

"You Don't Bring Me Flowers Anymore" (Barbra Streisand, Neil Diamond)

"You Don't Have To Be a Star" (Billy Davis, Jr. and Marilyn McCoo)

"You Fill up My Senses" (Annie's Song) (John Denver)

"You Light up My Life" (Debbie Boone)

"You Make Me So Very Happy" (Blood, Sweat and Tears)

"You Needed Me" (Anne Murray))

Check out these words. We often sang this to each other; it was true for both of us; we both felt rescued.

"You Raise Me Up" (Celtic Woman)

These lyrics are so touching and fitting for both of us.

"You Were Always on My Mind" (Willie Nelson)

"You'll Be in My Heart Always" (Phil Collins)

For anyone who is skeptical about what I'm relating about Mary Lee in this book, just look up the lyrics of this song and read them thoughtfully . . . it isn't "just all in my mind" as a coping mechanism.

"You'll Never Find" (Michael Boublez)

"Your Love Has Lifted Me Higher than I've ever been lifted before" (Rita Coolidge)

"You're Every Woman in the World" (Air Supply)

"You're in My Heart, You're in My Mind" (Rod Stewart)

"You're My Home" (Helen Reddy)

This text is so appropriate for early in our relationship; We always felt we were "at home" anywhere, as long as we were together.

"You're Nobody 'Til Somebody Loves You" (Dean Martin) (Michael Boublez)

"You're the Best Thing That Ever Happened to Me" (Gladys Knight and the Pips)

PIANO SONGS SHE HAS GIVEN TO ME

I was a piano major in college, and she knows I enjoy piano music.

"Allegro, Opus 8" by Robert Schumann

From the classical station I sometimes listen to.

"Autumn Leaves" (Roger Williams)

"Canadian Sunset" (Hugo Winterhalter)

In high school, I taught myself to play this, from a 45 rpm record.

"Polanaise No.3, Opus 53-"Heroic" by Fredric Chopin.

A song Mom used to play when we were little kids.

And several others I've enjoyed, but didn't know their titles.

SONGS GIVEN LATER,
AS SHE PREPARED TO "CROSS OVER"

"Baby, Baby, Don't Get Hooked on Me"
These first two were not very subtle "hints" to me.
"Breakin' Up Is So Hard to Do" (Neil Sedaka)
"Carry On"
Lots of positive energy, upbeat, sounds Celtic; words and music are encouraging.
"Everything Has Changed"(Taylor Swift)
"I Always Thought That I'd See You Again" (James Taylor)
"I Never Can Say Goodbye, Girl" (Jackson 5)
"My Universe Will Never Be the Same" (The Wanted)
"Someday We'll Be Together" (Diana Ross and the Supremes)
"There Ain't No Gettin' Over Me" (Ronnie Milsap)
This one made me laugh when I heard it!
"Whenever You Need Me, I'll Be There"(The Spinners)
"You Know You Love Her When You Let Her Go" (Passenger)
This song stunned me when I first heard it!
I released her a second time, as I had previously, in the hospital. Just before she left, she sent me 7 or 8 songs in a row, assuring me that she'd be "checking in on me from time to time."
The last song she sent me, as I arrived at my destination that day, was the song that had been the very first song she had sent me two years earlier:
"Lady" ("My Sweet Lady") (John Denver)
The words were about my tears, and a promise that our time together was not over . . . I wept.

    She moved on to a different realm, and the following Monday, the "oldies" station that had given us so many of the songs listed on the previous pages, was suddenly no longer in existence! Without notice, they had tossed the songs for us older folks and now had a new format, with younger DJs—they still called it an "oldies" station, but now it was for a generation twenty years younger!

    So, I looked around a found a couple of "acceptable" stations with newer songs and artists, with more interesting music and often more meaningful words.

    And even later, after I'd adjusted to her moving on.

    She began to send me new songs, from my "new" station, for instance:

"*. . . I swear to God I'm a one-woman lover, can't ever look at another . . ." (from a "country" station)*

    I'd never heard this song before, don't know what it is, but this line made me know that it's absolutely true for me. If I were to leave this life in about ten years, we'll celebrate our Golden Anniversary together!

    Who'da thunk it?

    As I had said to Mary Lee several years ago, "Why in the world would I even think about being with someone else, when I already have the *best* there is?"

    These are some of my favorites I often hear and enjoy these days:

"All of Me Loves All of You" (John Legend)
I still get all soft inside when I hear it and sing it.
This is a very tender love song, which I'm learning to sing. During one of my days with lots of appointments, beginning just as I started my car in the garage, until I finally pulled back in hours later, she had "given" it to me four times! It seems to have become our "new love song"—she sends it to me often, and I love it!
"As Long As I'm with You, There's No Place I'd Rather Be" (Clean Bandit- ft. Jess Glynne)
"At Last"(Etta James)
"Ain't It Fun" (Paramore)
This song has good energy, but (I recently discovered) it also has a sarcastic text.
I always enjoyed the music, but then I "Googled" the lyrics, and found that they're really pretty mean, directed at an "ex" (how do you like that, you stinker?)
It seems like the composer was venting a lot of anger when they wrote this,
but the words are somewhat hard to understand, and the music sounds . . . fun!
"Because I'm Happy" (Pharrell Williams)
I used to turn this song off, because except for the soloist, it was so repetitive and boring to me; but eventually, I began to pay close attention to the intricacies of the shifting harmonies and complex entrances and exits of the backup singers, and the polyrhythmic clapping—so now I'm intrigued enough to listen.
Do I sound like a music snob? Ok, sometimes, yeah.

"Bubbly" (Colbie Caillat)
Look up these words and listen—very upbeat and sweet, a wonderful message!
"Every Move You Make . . . I'll Be Watchin' You" (The Police)
"For the Longest Time" (Billy Joel)
"Girls Chase Boys Chase Girls" (Ingrid Michaelson)
"I Belong with You, You Belong with Me, You're My Sweetheart . . ." ("Ho Hey") (The Lumineers)
The chorus especially is a very upbeat, happy song.
"I Got a Peaceful, Easy Feeling" (Eagles)
"I Love You Just the Way You Are" (Billy Joel)
"I Should Have Brought You Flowers" (Bruno Mars)
"I Will Remember You" (Sarah McLachlan)
"In the Arms of an Angel" (Sarah McLachlan)
"I Will Wait, I Will Wait for You" (Mumford & Sons) *Words from her, to me—one of my favorites!*
"I Won't Give Up on Us" (Jason Mrraz)
Wonderful, spiritual words!
"I'm a Single Lady" (Beyonce)
I love the feisty energy of this song!
"I'm Gonna Make This Place Your Home" (Phillip Phillips)
"I'm Yours" (Jason Mraz)
Look up these great lyrics! Very upbeat and light-hearted—and funny lyrics!
"It's All Coming Back to Me Now" (Celine Dion)
"I've Loved You for a Thousand Years" (Christina Perri)
"Let It Go" (from the movie *Frozen*)(Idina Mensel)
I received this song when I started my car, after having an intensive session with Tina about letting go of something in my life that "no longer serves me well."
"Little Talks" (Of Monsters and Men)
Very interesting lyrics, even metaphysical.
"My Immortal" (Evanescence)
The lyrics are somewhat wrenching.
This song was given to me later, but it fits in with the deep despair and grief I had experienced twice—not long after her death, because for several weeks, I thought that she was gone from me forever.
"Never Gonna Dance Again the Way I Danced with You" (George Michael)
"Oh, Ho, Ho It's Magic" (Pilot)
"On the Wings of Love" (Jeffrey Osborne)
"Slow Dancin, Swayin, to the Music" (Johnny Rivers)

"Some People Wait a Lifetime for a Moment Like This" (Kelly Clarkson)
"Story of My Life" (One Direction)
Title only: Do ya' think?
"This Is Gonna Be the Best Day of My Life . . . Please Don't Wake Me Now" (American Authors)
Mary Lee often "gives" me this one, and I'm finding that more and more, that this IS the way I feel about this day being a "best day" for me. I'm learning to look at life – people and circumstances – from a more positive viewpoint. and you might be surprised at how much better your life can be from doing that.
Words of wisdom: "Thoughts held in mind produce after their own kind."
Translation: whatever part of your life that you "feed" (or dwell on) whether it's positive or negative, tends to grow.

"Tonight, I'm Gonna Hold You So Close" (Maroon 5)
"You Take My Breath Away" (Berlin)
"You're Amazing Just the Way You Are" (Bruno Mars)
"You're Still the One" (Shania Twain)
"We Can Learn to Love Again" (Pink)
"Wherever you go, whatever you do, I Will Be Right Here Waiting for You" (Richard Marx)
Mainly, the words in the chorus.
"Would You Know My Name, If I saw You in Heaven?" (would you hold my hand . . .) (Eric Clapton)
written after the death of his 5-year old son."
"You Are the Woman that I've always dreamed of . . . I knew it from the start" (Firefall)
"You're Gonna Miss Me When I'm Gone" (Anna Kendrick)
Fun song!
I laughed and agreed with her, that I did miss watching her walk and hearing her talk—and sing. You need to watch her "cup" version on You Tube, to get the full effect!
"You're So Vain" (Carly Simon)
"You're the One That I Love" (from *Grease*) (John Travolta and Olivia Newton John)
"You've Got a Friend" (James Taylor)

I'm going to continue to enjoy the songs she sends me from now on, but I won't be writing them down for this book; it's already a long enough chapter!

Recommended Reading

Note: All of these books are in our library, and most of them I have read. They are listed in the order I came in contact with them over the years. However, if it has an * in front of the title, I may have begun to read it at an earlier time but never finished it—or I may not have read it yet. As soon as this book is published, I intend to sit down and get acquainted (or re-acquainted) with each book listed that I haven't read recently. It's taken me years to get where I am now.

The Bible
. . . but not just any Bible. Find a "red-letter" edition, which has everything that Jesus himself said, shown in red ink. Now, read everything that Jesus said, and be sure to pay attention to what he DIDN'T say. (Judgmentalism, condemnation, so-and-so is going to hell, etc.—In the book of John, Ch. 8, Verse15, Jesus said: "I am not judging anyone." Notice what he said about the religious leaders of his day. (Guess why they had him killed?)

The Gospel of Thomas
It has many of Jesus's teachings in it; you can probably find it in your public library.

You Can Heal Your Life by Louise Hay
Learn to love, appreciate, and honor yourself...where you are NOW.

Seat of the Soul by Gary Zukav
This is the "earth school," we're here to learn.

**Soul Stories* by Gary Zukav
Follow-up stories.

**The Case for Reincarnation* (1986) by James Dillet Freeman
Dei J'a Vous? This seems like a dream I've had before . . .

**The Gift of Change* by Marianne Williamson
Every change is a challenge to become who we really are.

**Anatomy of the Spirit* by Caroline Myss, PH.D
Seven stages of cultivating your higher consciousness and physical wholeness.

Soul Retrieval by Sandra Ingerman
Sometimes, in order to survive, a part of our soul leaves us.

**Welcome Home* by Sandra Ingerman
The "follow-up": after part of our soul has returned to you.

The Secret by Rhonda Byrne
The book was written in 2006, and later was made into a movie.

> To find someone in your area who can help you with Shamanism, Google: www.shamanicteachers.com

Life After Life (late 1970's) by Raymond A. Moody, Jr., MD
   Through special hypnosis, we can remember a past life which may affect us now.

Reflections on "Life After Life" by Raymond A. Moody, Jr., MD
   A follow-up on his earlier research.

Journey of Souls (Life Between Lives) 1994 by Michael Newton, PH.D
   The spirit world is incredibly organized, rational, and we continue to learn & grow there.

Destiny of Souls (2001) by Michael Newton, PH.D
   His follow-up book.

Memories of the Afterlife by Michael Newton, PH.D
   Tina Zion wrote chapter 29 of his third book.

Stepping Through the Narrow Gate by Berry Vennard
   Evolutionary change happening to humans now is in the realm of consciousness.

Many Lives, Many Masters (1988) by Dr. Brian Weiss
   There are loving souls who can teach, guide, and protect us in this life..

Miracles Happen (2012) by Dr. Brian Weiss
   Written very recently.

Proof of Heaven by Dr. Alexander Eben
Neurosurgeon, didn't believe in afterlife—until he was in a coma and experienced it.

The Daily Word—a devotional publication of Unity
If interested, see subscription information; it's extremely positive and inspiring.

Daily Word
A Unity Publication
1901 NW Blue Parkway
Unity Village, MO 64065-0001
http://www.unity.org
1-800-669-0282

Also, if you're interested, find a local Unity Church or Spiritual Center; attend it several times (maybe with a friend?) and see if you feel at home with their inclusiveness and their acceptance of you and wherever you are on your spiritual path. It just may enrich the rest of your life from now on.)

ALSO:

Movie/DVD: *What Dreams May Come*
Starring Robin Williams, Cuba Gooding Jr, Max von Sydow.
Based on the novel by Richard Matheson and considered the most spiritual film ever done by Robin Williams.

It includes love, death, grieving, fear of interaction from the other side, suicide, the afterlife with other loving spirits, heaven, a kind of limbo with nothing but depression and utter hopelessness. The power of love and sacrifice, rescue, shared afterlife, including "we can do it better . . ." and even re-incarnation!

Rent it, borrow it, buy it, watch it!

CPSIA information can be obtained at www.ICGtesting.com
Printed in the USA
LVOW05s0019030715

444780LV00004B/5/P